Air Jordan Pi

(2013)

Michael Fox Steven Fox

Introduction

As the Air Jordan sneaker community continues to grow, finding a reliable source for current market values is becoming more difficult. It has become a widely spread problem as buyers and sellers search for the most accurate prices available. As a result, this book was born. We hope to ease your journey into the process of collecting, buying, and selling Air Jordans.

A significant amount of time and research was dedicated to the creation of this book. This valuable resource will best serve anyone with a desire to learn more about Jordans, avoid overpriced sneakers, selling for a fair price or perhaps make a cool profit—whatever the reason, use this guide wisely.

For the investment-minded collectors, the prices in this book are only a guide to what the items are worth in the secondary market. The market can often fluctuate due to current marketing trends. Because of that, we'll continue to update the prices in future editions of this book in order to provide you with the most up-to-date information available.

The prices listed in this guide are references made from reviewing eBay and online forums, as well as personal selling experiences. These prices are not based on what we or anyone assumes what a particular shoe is worth, but the average price a majority of the consumers will buy it for. Few will buy high and many will buy low, but the majority will eventually have to buy in between. That's the "average" price we are searching for.

To make this guide visually appealing, as well as interesting to read, this book consists of fun facts, quotes, and high quality photos. We are attempting to produce the best Jordan price guide, in the hopes of reaching out to casual fans and hard-core collectors alike. We hope you will gain many new insights, but more importantly, have fun along the way. Enjoy!

Disclaimer/Acknowledgment

Disclaimer :

All of the information, including valuations, in this book have been compiled from the most reliable sources, and every effort has been made to elimiate errors and questionable data.

Nevertheless, the possibility of error, in a work of such immense scope, always exist. The publisher or author will not be held responsible for losses which may occur during purchases, sales, or transaction of items, because of the information herein.

Readers who feel they have discovered errors are invited to write and inform us, so they may be corrected in subsequent editions. We are not affilated with the Jordan brand.

Acknowlegment:

First and foremost, this book is dedicated to you Mom.
May you rest in peace.

A special thanks to my family and friends who encouraged me and pushed me to finish this guide. It took a lot of time and sacrifice to compile all the information that has gone into this book, but with their love and support, completing our book was made possible.
A special thanks to my girlfriend Rachel, for always believing in me when no one else did and to our friend Jason, for his tips and encouragment towards helping us push our book.

Thank you to the people we've met along the way through Craigslist, eBay, and may others who have contributed their sneakers to us and made it possible to add color and history to this guide- we thank you!

For those who have bought this book, we deeply appreciate your support and hope you found value in our uniquely created
Air Jordan Price Guide!
Enjoy!

How To Use This Guide

This guide is an identification and price guide to the Air Jordan sneakers produced between (1985-2012). The price suggested values reflect the current market trends. These prices are what the average consumer is willing to pay for a particular pair of sneakers and the average price buyers are willing to sell based on prices online, shops, craigslist, etc.

This book is organized chronologically by year, with the first release of the Air Jordan 1 (I) through Air Jordan 14 (XIV) – the most popular models. This is only the beginning-we hope with your support, we will be able to continue making the guides for the rest of the Air Jordan series in the future.

By following the chart, you must first understand what each category means:

Picture:	Name:	Shoe Box:	Colorway:	Release Date/Retail Price/ Release Type	Market Value for DS (2013)

Picture – This will entail a photo of the specific model of the designed sneaker. Photo.

Name: This indicates the official given name or nickname of the sneaker. For Ex. Air Jordan X "Chicagos"

Shoe Box – The original packaging or container used to house the sneakers.

Colorway – The colorway of a given model sneaker

Release Date: The confirmed date a pair of sneakers was made available for purchase.

Retail Price – A suggested value the manufacture recommends that the retailer sells the sneaker for. (Ex. In 1985, the Air Jordan 1's retail price was $65.)

Market Value for DS (2013) – Is the up to date average market value for a specific pair of Air Jordans in brand new and unworn condition for 2013.

Abbreviations/Terminology

(AJKO) – Air Jordan Knock Out
Bin 23 – A collection of special edition Air Jordans (I-XX3)
BHM – Black History Month
Bred – Black/Red Colorway
(CDP) – Countdown Pack
(DMP) – Defining Moments Pack
Doernbecher – Specific pairs designed by children undergoing treatment at the Doernbecher Pediatric Hospital in Portland
(DS) – Deadstock (Brand new and unworn condition)
DTRT – Do The Right Thing
FTLOTG – For the Love of the Game
(GMP) – Golden Moments Pack
(GR) – General Release
(GS) – Grade School Release
(I.E) – International Exclusive
(LS) – Lifestyle Release
Original – Original Release
P.E. - Player Edition
(PR) – Past Releases
(QF) – Quarter Finals
(QS) – Quickstrike Release
Quai 54 – The Jordan Brand Quai 54 International Streetball tournament
Retro – The re-release of an original pair
TXT – Textile
UNC – University of North Carolina
Undftd – Undefeated
(W) – Womens

Table of Contents

Introduction..I
Disclaimer/Acknowledgment.....................................II
How To Use This Guide...III
Abbreviation/Terminology.....................................IV
Air Jordan 1(I)..6
   (1985) Air Jordan 1 (I) Original............................7,8,9
   (1986) Air Jordan 1 (I) Original.............................10
   (1986) Air Jordan 1 (I) Original Low......................10
   (1994) Air Jordan 1 (I) Retro.................................11
   (2001) Air Jordan 1 (I) Retro (USA EDITION)........11,12
   (2001) Air Jordan 1 (I) Retro (JAPAN EDITION).....12,13
   (2002) Air Jordan 1 (I) Retro.................................13
   (2003) Air Jordan 1 (I) Retro (Patent Leather)......13,14
   (2004) Air Jordan 1 (I) Retro Low..........................14
   (2007) Air Jordan 1 (I) Retro...............................15,16
   (2007) Air Jordan 1 (I) Retro Low.....................16,17,18
   (2008) Air Jordan 1 (I) Retro.........................19,20,21,22
   (2009) Air Jordan 1 (I) Retro...............23,24,25,26,27,28
   (2010) Air Jordan 1 (I) Retro..........................29,30,31
   (2011) Air Jordan 1 (I) Retro................................32,33
   (2012) Air Jordan 1 (I) Retro............................34,35,36
Air Jordan 2 (II)..37
   (1986) Air Jordan 2 (II) Original............................38
   (1987) Air Jordan 2 (II) Original............................39
   (1994) Air Jordan 2 (II) Retro................................39
   (1994) Air Jordan 2 (II) Retro Low.........................39
   (2004) Air Jordan 2 (II) Retro...............................38,39
   (2004) Air Jordan 2 (II) Retro Low.........................40
   (2005) Air Jordan 2 (II) Retro Low.........................41
   (2007) Air Jordan 2 (II) Retro................................41
   (2008) Air Jordan 2 (II) Retro................................42
   (2010) Air Jordan 2 (II) Retro..............................42,43
Air Jordan 3 (III)...44

- (1988) Air Jordan 3 (III) Original..45
- (1994) Air Jordan 3 (III) Retro..46
- (2001) Air Jordan 3 (III) Retro..46
- (2003) Air Jordan 3 (III) Retro..47
- (2007) Air Jordan 3 (III) Retro..47,48
- (2008) Air Jordan 3 (III) Retro..49
- (2009) Air Jordan 3 (III) Retro..49
- (2010) Air Jordan 3 (III) Retro..50
- (2011) Air Jordan 3 (III) Retro..50,51

Air Jordan 4 (IV)..52
- (1989) Air Jordan 4 (IV) Original...53
- (1999) Air Jordan 4 (IV) Retro..54
- (2000) Air Jordan 4 (IV) Retro..55
- (2004) Air Jordan 4 (IV) Retro..55
- (2005) Air Jordan 4 (IV) Retro (L.E.)......................................56
- (2006) Air Jordan 4 (IV) Retro (L.E.)......................................57
- (2006) Air Jordan 4 (IV) Retro 57,58,59
- (2007) Air Jordan 4 (IV) Retro..59
- (2008) Air Jordan 4 (IV) Retro..59
- (2010) Air Jordan 4 (IV) Retro..60
- (2011) Air Jordan 4 (IV) Retro..60
- (2012) Air Jordan 4 (IV) Retro..60,61,62

Air Jordan 5 (V)...63
- (1990) Air Jordan 5 (V) Original..64
- (2000) Air Jordan 5 (V) Retro...65
- (2006) Air Jordan 5 (V) Retro..65,66,67
- (2007) Air Jordan 5 (V) Retro..67,68
- (2007) Air Jordan 5 (V) Retro Low...68
- (2008) Air Jordan 5 (V) Retro...69
- (2011) Air Jordan 5 (V) Retro..70,71

Air Jordan 6 (VI)..72
- (1990) Air Jordan 6 (VI) Original...73
- (1991) Air Jordan 6 (VI) Original..73,74
- (2000) Air Jordan 6 (VI) Retro..74

(2002) Air Jordan 6 (VI) Retro Low............................ 75
(2006) Air Jordan 6 (VI) Retro...............................75
(2008) Air Jordan 6 (VI) Retro...............................76
(2009) Air Jordan 6 (VI) Retro...............................76
(2010) Air Jordan 6 (VI) Retro............................ 77,78
(2012) Air Jordan 6 (VI) Retro............................ 78,79
Air Jordan 7 (VII).. 80
(1991) Air Jordan 7 (VII) Original........................... 81
(1992) Air Jordan 7 (VII) Original...........................81,82
(2002) Air Jordan 7 (VII) Retro............................. 82
(2004) Air Jordan 7 (VII) Retro............................. 83
(2006) Air Jordan 7 (VII) Retro........................... 83,84
(2008) Air Jordan 7 (VII) Retro........................... 84,85
(2009) Air Jordan 7 (VII) Retro............................. 85
(2010) Air Jordan 7 (VII) Retro............................. 86
(2011) Air Jordan 7 (VII) Retro...........................86,87
(2012) Air Jordan 7 (VII) Retro...........................87,88
Air Jordan 8 (VIII)..89
(1993) Air Jordan 8 (VIII) Original..........................90
(2003) Air Jordan 8 (VIII) Retro............................90,91
(2003) Air Jordan 8 (VIII) Retro Low......................... 91
(2007) Air Jordan 8 (VIII) Retro............................92,92
(2007) Air Jordan 8 (VIII) Retro Low......................... 93
(2008) Air Jordan 8 (VIII) Retro.............................94
Air Jordan 9 (IX).. 95
(1993) Air Jordan 9 (IX) Original............................ 96
(1994) Air Jordan 9 (IX) Original............................ 96
(2002) Air Jordan 9 (IX) Retro............................... 97
(2002) Air Jordan 9 (IX) Retro Low........................ 97,98
(2008) Air Jordan 9 (IX) Retro............................... 98
(2010) Air Jordan 9 (IX) Retro...................... 98,99,100
(2012) Air Jordan 9 (IX) Retro............................101,102
Air Jordan 10 (X)..103
(1994) Air Jordan 10 (X) Original........................... 104

(1995) Air Jordan 10 (X) Original..........................104,105
(2005) Air Jordan 10 (X) Retro.............................106,107
(2008) Air Jordan 10 (X) Retro................................107
(2012) Air Jordan 10 (X) Retro................................108

Air Jordan 11 (XI).. 109
(1995) Air Jordan 11 (XI) Original.............................110
(1996) Air Jordan 11 (XI) Original.............................110
(1996) Air Jordan 11 (XI) Original Low.........................111
(2000) Air Jordan 11 (XI) Retro................................111
(2001) Air Jordan 11 (XI) Retro................................112
(2001) Air Jordan 11 (XI) Retro Low.......................112,113
(2003) Air Jordan 11 (XI) Retro Low............................114
(2006) Air Jordan 11 (XI) Retro................................114
(2007) Air Jordan 11 (XI) Retro Low.......................115,116
(2008) Air Jordan 11 (XI) Retro................................116
(2009) Air Jordan 11 (XI) Retro................................117
(2010) Air Jordan 11 (XI) Retro................................117
(2011) Air Jordan 11 (XI) Retro Low............................118
(2011) Air Jordan 11 (XI) Retro................................118
(2012) Air Jordan 11 (XI) Retro................................119

Air Jordan 12 (XII)... 120
(1996) Air Jordan 12 (XII) Original............................121
(1997) Air Jordan 12 (XII) Original.......................121,122
(2003) Air Jordan 12 (XII) Retro...............................122
(2004) Air Jordan 12 (XII) Retro...............................123
(2004) Air Jordan 12 (XII) Retro Low......................123,124
(2008) Air Jordan 12 (XII) Retro...............................124
(2009) Air Jordan 12 (XII) Retro...............................125
(2011) Air Jordan 12 (XII) Retro Low...........................126
(2012) Air Jordan 12 (XII)................................126,127

Air Jordan 13 (XIII)..128
(1997) Air Jordan 13 (XIII) Original...........................129
(1998) Air Jordan 13 (XIII) Original......................129,130
(1998) Air Jordan 13 (XIII) Original Low.......................131

(2004) Air Jordan 13 (XIII) Retro..........................130,131
(2005) Air Jordan 13 (XIII) Retro..........................131,132
(2005) Air Jordan 13 (XIII) Retro Low.................. 132,133
(2008) Air Jordan 13 (XIII) Retro.............................. 134
(2010) Air Jordan 13 (XIII) Retro..........................134,135
(2011) Air Jordan 13 (XIII) Retro....................... 135,136

Air Jordan 14 (XIV)... 137
   (1998) Air Jordan 14 (XIV) Original........................... 138
   (1999) Air Jordan 14 (XIV) Original..................... 138,139
   (1999) Air Jordan 14 (XIV) Original Low..................... 139
   (2005) Air Jordan 14 (XIV) Retro..........................140,141
   (2006) Air Jordan 14 (XIV) Retro.............................. 142
   (2006) Air Jordan 14 (XIV) Retro Low.................. 142,143
   (2008) Air Jordan 14 (XIV) Retro.............................. 143
   (2011) Air Jordan 14 (XIV) Retro..........................143,144
   (2012) Air Jordan 14 (XIV) Retro..........................144,145

Air Jordan Packages... 146
   BMP "Beginning Moments Pack"................................ 146
   CDP "Countdown Pack"..........................146,147,148,149
   DMP "Defining Moments Pack"...........................149,150
   GMP "Golden Moments Pack"................................. 151
   Air Jordan Infrared Pack... 151

AIR JORDAN 1 (I)

Air Jordan 1 (I)

The Air Jordan 1 (I)'s were the first Air Jordan released by Nike and were created by Nike's head designer, Peter Moore. The Air Jordan 1 (I) were considered a breakthrough due to its unique basketball shoe design and the many colorways it featured.

The lack of the color white on the shoe stirred much controversy with NBA commissioner, David Stern. The shoes were considered a violation of on-court dress code and were banned from NBA courts. However, Michael continued to wear the shoes and was fined each time he wore them during games.

(1985) Air Jordan 1 (I) Original

Picture:	Name:	Shoe Box:	Colorway:	Release Date/Retail Price/ Release Type	Market Value for DS (2013)
#1	Air Jordan 1 (I) Original High "Banned"		Black/Red	06/1985 $65 GR	$1,500 +
#2	Air Jordan 1 (I) Original High "Bulls"		White/Black-Red	06/1985 $65 GR	$1,500 +
#3	Air Jordan 1 (I) Original High "Black Toe"		White/Black-Red	10/1985 $65 N/A	$1,450 +
#4	Air Jordan 1 (I) Original High "Royal Blue"		Black/Royal-Blue	1985 $65 GR	$1,000 +
#5	Air Jordan 1 (I) Original High "AJKO"		White/Black-Red	1985 N/A N/A	$1,300 +

Quote:

"I've always believed that if you put in work, the results will come."

-Michael Jordan

(1985) Air Jordan 1 (I) Original

Picture:	Name:	Shoe Box:	Colorway:	Release Date/Retail Price/ Release Type	Market Value for DS (2013)
#6	Air Jordan 1 (I) Original High		Black/Soft Grey	1985 $65 GR	$1,200 +
#7	Air Jordan 1 (I) Original High		White/Natural Grey	1985 $65 GR	$950 +

(1985) Air Jordan 1 (I) Original

Picture:	Name:	Shoe Box:	Colorway:	Release Date/Retail Price/ Release Type	Market Value for DS (2013)
#8	Air Jordan 1 (I) Original High		White/Blue	1985 $65 N/A	$900 +
#9	Air Jordan 1 (I) Original High		White/Black	1985 $65 N/A	$850 +

(1985) Air Jordan 1 (I) Original

Picture:	Name:	Shoe Box:	Colorway:	Release Date/Retail Price/ Release Type	Market Value for DS (2013)
#10	Air Jordan 1 (I) Original High "UNC"		White/ Carolina Blue	1985 $65 N/A	$800 +
#11	Air Jordan 1 (I) Original High "Metallic Blue"		White/ Metallic Blue	1985 $65 N/A	$1,500 +
#12	Air Jordan 1 (I) Original High "Metallic Orange"		White/ Metallic Orange	1985 $65 N/A	$1,200 +
#13	Air Jordan 1 (I) Original High "Metallic Green"		White/ Metallic Green	1985 $65 N/A	$1,500 +
#14	Air Jordan 1 (I) Original High "Metallic Red"		White/ Metallic Dark Red	1985 $65 N/A	$1,100 +
#15	Air Jordan 1 (I) Original High "Metallic Purple"		White/ Metallic Purple	1985 $65 N/A	$1,400 +

(1986) Air Jordan 1 (I) Original

Picture:	Name:	Shoe Box:	Colorway:	Release Date/Retail Price/ Release Type	Market Value for DS (2013)
#16	Air Jordan 1 (I) Original AJKO "Bred"		Black/Red	1986 N/A N/A	$1,300 +

(1986) Air Jordan 1 (I) Original Low

Picture:	Name:	Shoe Box:	Colorway:	Release Date/Retail Price/ Release Type	Market Value for DS (2013)
#17	Air Jordan 1 (I) Original Low		White/Metallic Blue	1986 $64.99 GR	$1,300 +
#18	Air Jordan 1 (I) Original Low		White/Natural Grey	1986 $64.99 GR	$1,000 +
N/A #19	Air Jordan 1 (I) Original Low		White/Dark-Red	1986 $64.99 GR	$1,350 +

Fun Fact:

Michael Jordan was born on February 17th, 1963.

(1994) Air Jordan 1 (I) Retro

Picture:	Name:	Shoe Box:	Colorway:	Release Date/Retail Price/ Release Type	Market Value for DS (2013)
#20	Air Jordan 1 (I) Retro High "Chicago Bulls" (PR:'85)		White/Black - Red	1994 $80 GR	$580-$600
#21	Air Jordan 1 (I) Retro High "Banned" (PR:'85)		Black/Red	1994 $80 GR	$580-$620

(2001) Air Jordan 1 (I) Retro (USA Edition)

Picture:	Name:	Shoe Box:	Colorway:	Release Date/Retail Price/ Release Type	Market Value for DS (2013)
#22	Air Jordan 1 (I) Retro High "Banned" (PR: '85, '94)		Black/ Varsity - Red	08/25/2001 $80 GR	$520-$550

Fact:

Michael Jordan scored over 30,000 points in his career.

(2001) Air Jordan 1 (I) Retro (USA Edition)

Picture:	Name:	Shoe Box:	Colorway:	Release Date/Retail Price/ Release Type	Market Value for DS (2013)
#23	Air Jordan 1 (I) Retro High "Royal Blue" (PR: '85)		Black/ Varsity Royal Blue - White	10/06/2001 $80 GR	**$480-$520**
#24	Air Jordan 1 (I) Retro High "Midnight Navy"		White/ Metallic Silver - Midnight Navy	08/25/2001 $80 GR	**$220-$240**

(2001) Air Jordan 1 (I) Retro (Japan Edition)

Picture:	Name:	Shoe Box:	Colorway:	Release Date/Retail Price/ Release Type	Market Value for DS (2013)
#25	Air Jordan 1 (I) Retro High		White/ White-Midnight Navy	08/13/2001 12,000 Yen ($117) Japan Release only	**$170-$190**
#26	Air Jordan 1 (I) Retro High		Black/Black -Metallic Silver	10/4/2001 12,000 Yen ($117) Japan Release only	**$270-$300**

(2001) Air Jordan 1 (I) Retro (Japan Edition)

Picture:	Name:	Shoe Box:	Colorway:	Release Date/Retail Price/ Release Type	Market Value for DS (2013)
 #27	Air Jordan 1 (I) Retro High		Neutral Grey/Silver-White	10/06/2001 12,000 Yen ($117) Japan Release only	$180-$200

(2002) Air Jordan 1 (I) Retro

Picture:	Name:	Shoe Box:	Colorway:	Release Date/Retail Price/ Release Type	Market Value for DS (2013)
 #28	Air Jordan 1 (I) Retro High		White/ Metallic Silver	12/26/2002 $100 GR	$80-$100

(2003) Air Jordan 1 (I) Retro (Patent Leather)

Picture:	Name:	Shoe Box:	Colorway:	Release Date/Retail Price/ Release Type	Market Value for DS (2013)
 #29	Air Jordan 1 (I) Retro High "UNC"		White/ Carolina Blue	09/27/2003 $100 GR	$220-$240

(2003) Air Jordan 1 (I) Retro (Patent Leather)

Picture:	Name:	Shoe Box:	Colorway:	Release Date/Retail Price/ Release Type	Market Value for DS (2013)
#30	Air Jordan 1 (I) Retro High "Bulls" (PR: '85, '94)		White/Black Varsity-Red	11/22/2003 $100 GR	$240-$270
#31	Air Jordan 1 (I) Retro High "Metallic Gold"		Black/ Metallic Gold	12/23/2003 $100 GR	$260-$280

(2004) Air Jordan 1 (I) Retro Low

Picture:	Name:	Shoe Box:	Colorway:	Release Date/Retail Price/ Release Type	Market Value for DS (2013)
#32	Air Jordan 1 (I) Retro Low		White/ White/ Metallic Silver	06/12/2004 $100 GR	$70-$90
#33	Air Jordan 1 (I) Retro Low		White/ Metallic Silver/ Midnight Navy	06/12/2004 $80 GR	$50-$60

(2007) Air Jordan 1 (I) Retro

Picture:	Name:	Shoe Box:	Colorway:	Release Date/Retail Price/ Release Type	Market Value for DS (2013)
#34	Air Jordan 1 (I) Retro High "Old Love-Blacktoe" (PR: '85)		White/Black - Varsity Red	04/21/2007 $200 for pack Limited Release	$200-$230
#35	Air Jordan 1 (I) Retro High "New Love"		Black/ Varsity-Maize/ White	04/21/2007 $200 for pack Limited Release	$190-$220

(2007) Air Jordan 1 (I) Retro

Picture:	Name:	Shoe Box:	Colorway:	Release Date/Retail Price/ Release Type	Market Value for DS (2013)
#36	Air Jordan 1 (I) Retro High (LS) "Undftd 2"		Stealth/ Varsity Royal - Sport Red	05/19/2007 $110 Limited-Release	$80-$90
#37	Air Jordan 1 (I) Retro High (LS) "Undftd"		Sport Red/ White - Varsity Red	05/19/2007 $110 Limited-Release	$150-$160

(2007) Air Jordan 1 (I) Retro

Picture:	Name:	Shoe Box:	Colorway:	Release Date/Retail Price/ Release Type	Market Value for DS (2013)
#38	Air Jordan 1 (I) Retro High "Alpha"		Alpha University Blue/White - Black	06/02/2007 $110 GR	**$120-$140**
#39	Air Jordan 1 (I) Retro High "China"		White/Gold Dust – Sport Red - Black	06/01/2007 $205 Limited to China only	**$500+**

(2007) Air Jordan 1 (I) Retro Low

Picture:	Name:	Shoe Box:	Colorway:	Release Date/Retail Price/ Release Type	Market Value for DS (2013)
#40	Air Jordan 1 (I) Retro Low "Crocodile Pure"		White/ Metallic Silver – White Crocodile Pure	11/2007 $100 Limited Release	**$100-$110**
#41	Air Jordan 1 (I) Retro Low "Crocodile Pure"		Black/ Metallic Silver - Black	11/2007 $100 Limited Release	**$110-$120**

(2007) Air Jordan 1 (I) Retro Low

Picture:	Name:	Shoe Box:	Colorway:	Release Date/Retail Price/Release Type	Market Value for DS (2013)
#42	Air Jordan 1 (I) Retro Low "Inline"		Black/Metallic Silver - Varsity Red	05/26/2007 $90 GR	$80-$90
#43	Air Jordan 1 (I) Retro Low "West"		White/Chlorine Blue - Sonic Yellow	05/26/2007 $90 Regional Release (CA, AZ)	$60-$80
#44	Air Jordan 1 (I) Retro Low "East"		White/Varsity Red - Varsity Royal	05/26/2007 $90 Regional Release	$90-$110

(2007) Air Jordan 1 (I) Retro Low

Picture:	Name:	Shoe Box:	Colorway:	Release Date/Retail Price/Release Type	Market Value for DS (2013)
 #45	Air Jordan 1 (I) Retro Low "North"		White/Dark Forest - Light Graphite	05/26/2007 $90 Regional Release	$70-$90

(2007) Air Jordan 1 (I) Retro Low

Picture:	Name:	Shoe Box:	Colorway:	Release Date/Retail Price/ Release Type	Market Value for DS (2013)
 #46	Air Jordan 1 (I) Retro Low "South"		True White/ Varsity Red Stealth	05/26/2007 $90 Regional Release	$80-$100

(2007) Air Jordan 1 (I) Retro Low

Picture:	Name:	Shoe Box:	Colorway:	Release Date/Retail Price/ Release Type	Market Value for DS (2013)
 #47	(W) Air Jordan 1 (I) Retro Low		Denim/ White - Sport Red	05/19/2007 $85 GR-Women	$60-$75
 #48	(W) Air Jordan 1 (I) Retro Low		White/ Denim	05/19/2007 $85 GR-Women	$70-$80

Fun Fact:
Michael Jordan was born in Brooklyn, New York.

(2008) Air Jordan 1 (I) Retro

Picture:	Name:	Shoe Box:	Colorway:	Release Date/Retail Price/Release Type	Market Value for DS (2013)
#49	Air Jordan 1 (I) Retro High 23/501 "Levi Denim"		Varsity Red/ Midnight Navy-khaki-White	03/15/2008 $310 Limited Release	$700+
#50	Air Jordan 1 (I) Retro High "Opening Day Away"		Black/ White/Silver – Dark Charcoal	04/05/2008 $100 Limited Release	$100-$120

(2008) Air Jordan 1 (I) Retro

Picture:	Name:	Shoe Box:	Colorway:	Release Date/Retail Price/Release Type	Market Value for DS (2013)
#51	Air Jordan 1 (I) Retro High "Opening Day Home"		White/Black -Silver	04/05/2008 $100 Limited Release	$100-$120
#52	(GS) Air Jordan 1 (I) Retro High		Emerald Green/Black -Grape	05/2008 $75 GR- (GS)	$80-$90

(2008) Air Jordan 1 (I) Retro

Picture:	Name:	Shoe Box:	Colorway:	Release Date/Retail Price/ Release Type	Market Value for DS (2013)
#53	Air Jordan 1 (I) Retro High "Army Edition"		Pearl White/Hay-Walnut	05/24/2008 $100 GR	**$80-$100**
#54	Air Jordan 1 (I) Retro High "Army Edition"		Medium Brown/ Urban Haze-Hay-Anthracite	05/24/2008 $100 GR	**$150-$180**

(2008) Air Jordan 1 (I) Retro

Picture:	Name:	Shoe Box:	Colorway:	Release Date/Retail Price/ Release Type	Market Value for DS (2013)
#55	Air Jordan 1 (I) Retro High "Father's Day"		Black/White	06/07/2008 $100 GR	**$130-$150**
#56	Air Jordan 1 (I) Retro High "Father's Day"		White/Dark Charcoal-Tweed-Varsity-Red	06/07/2008 $100 GR	**$120-$140**

(2008) Air Jordan 1 (I) Retro

Picture:	Name:	Shoe Box:	Colorway:	Release Date/Retail Price/ Release Type	Market Value for DS (2013)
#57	Air Jordan 1 (I) Retro High "Olympic"		White/ Varsity Red- Midnight Navy- Metallic Gold	09/13/2008 $100 Limited Release	$130-$160
#58	Air Jordan 1 (I) Retro High (PR: '85)		High White/Black	09/20/2008 $310 Limited-Release	$180-$210

(2008) Air Jordan 1 (I) Retro

Picture:	Name:	Shoe Box:	Colorway:	Release Date/Retail Price/ Release Type	Market Value for DS (2013)
#59	Air Jordan 1 (I) Retro High		Varsity Red/Dark Army-White	11/08/2008 $115 GR	*$140-$170
#60	Air Jordan 1 (I) Retro High		Black/ Varsity Red- White	11/08/2008 $115 Limited Release	$140-$170

(2008) Air Jordan 1 (I) Retro

Picture:	Name:	Shoe Box:	Colorway:	Release Date/Retail Price/ Release Type	Market Value for DS (2013)
#61	Air Jordan 1 (I) Retro High Doernbecher		Black/Vivid Blue-White-Varsity Maize	11/14/2008 $125 Limited Release	$340 +
#62	Air Jordan 1 (I) Retro High Strap		Black/White - Varsity Red	11/22/08 $100 GR	$150-$170
#63	Air Jordan 1 (I) Retro High Strap		White/Black - Varsity Red	11/22/2008 $110 GR	$80-$100
#64	Air Jordan 1 (I) Retro High Strap		Black/White	11/22/2008 $110 GR	$80-$100

Quote:
"I never look at the consequences of missing a big shot…when you think of the consequences you always think of a negative result."

-Michael Jordan

(2009) Air Jordan 1 (I) Retro

Picture:	Name:	Shoe Box:	Colorway:	Release Date/Retail Price/ Release Type	Market Value for DS (2013)
#65	Air Jordan 1 (I) Retro High (QS)		Pewter/ Black -Max Orange	01/31/2009 $115 Limited- Release	$120-$140
#66	Air Jordan 1 (I) Retro High Strap Tribe Called Quest "Sole to Sole"		Black/ Varsity Red – Classic Green	02/2009 $110 Limited- Release	$130-$150
#67	Air Jordan 1 (I) Retro High "Max Orange"		Black/Max Orange - White	02/14/2009 $105 GR	$150-$180
#68	Air Jordan 1 (I) Retro High (LS)		Blue Sapphire/ Neon Turquoise -White	03/14/2009 $105 Limited Release	$90-$120
#69	Air Jordan 1 (I) Retro High Strap		Black/ University Blue - White	04/01/2009 $110 Limited- Release	$90-$100

(2009) Air Jordan 1 (I) Retro

Picture:	Name:	Shoe Box:	Colorway:	Release Date/Retail Price/ Release Type	Market Value for DS (2013)
#70	Air Jordan 1 (I) Retro High (LS) "Polka Dot"		Black/White	04/01/2009 $100 Limited-Release	$150-$170
#71	Air Jordan 1 (I) Retro High "Hare"		Light Silver/White-True Red	04/11/2009 $110 Limited-Release	$230-$260
#72	Air Jordan 1 (I) Retro High Strap		Midnight Navy/Varsity Red-Sail	05/01/2009 $110 GR	$130-$150
#73	Air Jordan 1 (I) Retro High		Black/Laser Blue	05/01/2009 $100 Limited-Release	$90-$110
#74	Air Jordan 1 (I) Retro High "Cinco de Mayo"		Black/White-Classic Green-Varsity Red	05/02/2009 $100 GR	$120-$140

(2009) Air Jordan 1 (I) Retro

Picture:	Name:	Shoe Box:	Colorway:	Release Date/Retail Price/ Release Type	Market Value for DS (2013)
#75	Air Jordan 1 (I) Retro High "Cinco de Mayo"		White/Black-Classic Green-Varsity Red	05/02/2009 $100 GR	$110-$130
#76	Air Jordan 1 (I) Retro High		Black/Chlorophyll	06/01/2009 $100 Limited-Release	$70-$80
#77	Air Jordan 1 (I) Retro High		Khaki/Hyper Verde-Midnight Navy	06/01/2009 $100 Limited-Release	$90-$110
#78	Air Jordan 1 (I) Retro High Quai 54 "Ruff N Tuff"		Laser Blue/Black White	06/11/2009 $125 Limited-Release (UK)	$180-$200
#79	Air Jordan 1 (I) Retro High DTRT Pack (PR: '85)		White/Varsity Red	07/04/2009 $105 Limited Release	$110-$120

(2009) Air Jordan 1 (I) Retro

Picture:	Name:	Shoe Box:	Colorway:	Release Date/Retail Price/ Release Type	Market Value for DS (2013)
#80	Air Jordan 1 (I) Retro High DTRT Pack (PR: '85)		White/Sea Green	07/04/2009 $105 Limited Release	**$110-$120**
#81	Air Jordan 1 (I) Retro High Strap		White/ Madeira-Ginger	08/01/2009 $110 GR	**$90-$110**
#82	Air Jordan 1 (I) Retro High Strap "Alpha/ Omega"		Grand Purple/ Varsity Maize-White	09/1/2009 $110 GR	**$65-$85**
#83	Air Jordan 1 (I) Retro High		Black/ Shadow Grey-White	09/01/2009 $110 GR	**$150-$180**

Quote:

"I failed over and over again in my life and that is why I succeed."

-Michael Jordan

(2009) Air Jordan 1 (I) Retro

Picture:	Name:	Shoe Box:	Colorway:	Release Date/Retail Price/ Release Type	Market Value for DS (2013)
#84	Air Jordan 1 (I) Retro High "Banned" (PR:'85,'94, '01)		Black/ Varsity Red	07/11/2009 $225 Pack Limited-Release	$270-$310
#85	Air Jordan 1 (I) Retro High "Boston"		White/Black -Celtic Green	07/11/2009 $225 Pack Limited-Release	$140-$160
#86	Air Jordan 1 (I) Retro High (PR: '85)		White/ Grand Purple	09/01/2009 $110 Limited-Release International	$120-$130
#87	Air Jordan 1 (I) Retro High Hall of Fame Pack		Black/ Metallic Gold-Varsity Red	09/05/2009 $125 Limited-Release	$100-$110
#88	Air Jordan 1 (I) Retro High (QS) "Leroy Smith"		Black/ Metallic Gold-Varsity Purple-Sport	10/31/2010 $125 Limited-Release	$120-$150

(2009) Air Jordan 1 (I) Retro

Picture:	Name:	Shoe Box:	Colorway:	Release Date/Retail Price/ Release Type	Market Value for DS (2013)
#89	Air Jordan 1 (I) Retro High Strap		Black/Black-Voltage Yellow	11/01/2009 $110 GR	$100-$120
#90	Air Jordan 1 (I) Retro High Strap		Black/Black-Orion	12/01/2009 $115 GR	$110-$130
#91	Air Jordan 1 (I) Retro High		Dark Obsidian/Dark Obsidian/White	12/01/2009 $110 GR	$80-$100
#92	Air Jordan 1 (I) Retro High		Metallic Zinc/Metallic Zinc/Shadow Grey	12/01/09 $110 GR	$80-$100

Did you know?

The Air Jordan 1 (I) was the most expensive basketball shoe on the market at the time of its release – retailing at $65.

(2010) Air Jordan 1 (I) Retro

Picture:	Name:	Shoe Box:	Colorway:	Release Date/Retail Price/ Release Type	Market Value for DS (2013)
#93	Air Jordan 1 (I) Retro High "Silver Anniversary"		Neutral Grey/ Metallic Silver	02/13/2010 $140 Limited-Release	**$150-$180**
#94	Air Jordan 1 (I) Retro High		Urban Haze/Dark Army-Bright Cactus	02/2010 $115 GR	**$90-$100**
#95	Air Jordan 1 (I) Retro High		Dark Obsidian/ Cerulean	032010 $115 GR	**$90-$100**
#96	Air Jordan 1 (I) High Retro KO (PR: '85)		White/Black-Varsity Red	03/27/2010 $125 Limited-Release	**$150-$180**
#97	Air Jordan 1 (I) High Retro KO		White/ Varsity Red	03/27/2010 $125 Limited-Release	**$130-$160**

(2010) Air Jordan 1 (I) Retro

Picture:	Name:	Shoe Box:	Colorway:	Release Date/Retail Price/ Release Type	Market Value for DS (2013)
#98	Air Jordan 1 (I) Retro Hi "A2K" (QS)		Multi-Colored	06/03/2010 N/A Limited-Release	$140-$160
#99	Air Jordan 1 (I) Retro High		Wolf Grey/Spice-White	07/2010 $110 GR	$110-$120
#100	Air Jordan 1 (I) Retro High		Black/Cyber-Black-Blue Sapphire	08/01/2011 $110 GR	$80-$100
#101	Air Jordan 1 (I) Retro High		Stealth/Team Red-Light Graphite-Charcoal	08//2010 $110 GR	$60-$80
#102	Air Jordan 1 (I) Retro High		Velvet Brown/Deep Garnet-Dark Sage-Light Chocolate	09/2/2010 $110 GR	$110-$130

(2010) Air Jordan 1 (I) Retro

Picture:	Name:	Shoe Box:	Colorway:	Release Date/Retail Price/ Release Type	Market Value for DS (2013)
#103	Air Jordan 1 (I) Retro Anodized		Metallic Silver/White	11//2010 $150 GR	**$80-$100**
#104	Air Jordan 1 (I) Retro Anodized		Varsity Red/Black-White	11/2010 $150 GR	**$50-$70**
#105	Air Jordan 1 (I) Retro Anodized		Black/ Anthracite	12/2010 $150 GR	**$80-$100**
#106	Air Jordan 1 (I) Retro Anodized		University Blue/Black-White	12/04/2010 $150 GR	**$60-$80**
#107	Air Jordan 1 (I) Retro Anodized		Altitude Green/Black	12/11/2010 $150 GR	**$60-$80**

(2011) Air Jordan 1 (I) Retro

Picture:	Name:	Shoe Box:	Colorway:	Release Date/Retail Price/Release Type	Market Value for DS (2013)
#108	Air Jordan 1 (I) Retro High "Banned" (PR:'85, '94,'01)		Black/Varsity Red-White	06/01/2011 06/04/2011 $125 Limited-Release	$560-$590
#109	Air Jordan 1 (I) Retro High Colors Pack		White/White-University Blue	08/06/2011 $110 Limited-Release	$100-$110
#110	Air Jordan 1 (I) Retro High Colors Pack		White/White-Pine Green	08/06/2011 $110 Limited-Release	$100-$110
#111	Air Jordan 1 (I) Retro High Colors Pack		White/White-Midnight Navy	08/06/2011 $110 Limited-Release	$100-$110
#112	Air Jordan 1 (I) Retro High Colors Pack		White/White-Varsity Red	08/06/2011 $110 Limited-Release	$100-$110

(2011) Air Jordan 1 (I) Retro

Picture:	Name:	Shoe Box:	Colorway:	Release Date/Retail Price/ Release Type	Market Value for DS (2013)
#113	Air Jordan 1 (I) Retro High Colors Pack		White/White-Varsity Maize	08/06/2011 $110 Limited-Release	$100-$110
#114	Air Jordan 1 (I) Retro High Colors Pack		White/White-Varsity Royal	08/06/2011 $110 Limited-Release	$100-$110
#115	Air Jordan 1 (I) Retro High KO		Light Graphite/Black-Varsity Red	11/15/2011 $130 Limited-Release	$100-$130
#116	Air Jordan 1 (I) Retro High KO		Dark Cinder/Black-Varsity Red	11/15/2011 $130 Limited-Release	$70-$100
#117	Air Jordan 1 (I) Retro High KO		Black/Anthracite-Varsity Red	11/15/2011 $130 Limited-Release	$130-$150

(2012) Air Jordan 1 (I) Retro

Picture:	Name:	Shoe Box:	Colorway:	Release Date/Retail Price/ Release Type	Market Value for DS (2013)
#118	Air Jordan 1 (I) Retro High "Dave"		Black/Sport Red-White-Cement Grey	02/11/2012 $175 Limited-Release	$200-$230
#119	Air Jordan 1 (I) Retro High "Las Vegas"		Black/Metallic Gold/White-Gym Red	07/07/12 $130 GR	$130-$160
#120	Air Jordan 1 (I) Retro High "Washington DC"		Obsidian/Metallic Gold-White	07/14/2012 $130 GR	$110-$130

(2012) Air Jordan 1 (I) Retro

Picture:	Name:	Shoe Box:	Colorway:	Release Date/Retail Price/ Release Type	Market Value for DS (2013)
#121	Air Jordan 1 (I) Retro High Strap Premier		White/White-Varsity Red-Midnight Navy	05/05/2012 $115 Limited-Release	$105-$120

(2012) Air Jordan 1 (I) Retro

Picture:	Name:	Shoe Box:	Colorway:	Release Date/Retail Price/Release Type	Market Value for DS (2013)
#122	Air Jordan 1 (I) Retro High Strap Premier (PR: '09)		Midnight Navy/Varsity Red-Sail	05/05/2012 $110 Limited-Release	$130-$150
#123	Air Jordan 1 (I) Retro High KO (QS) (PR: '86)		Black/Varsity Red-White	06/02/2012 $125 Limited-Release	$190-$220
#124	Air Jordan 1 (I) Retro High KO (QS) "Black Toe" (PR: '85)		White/Black-Varsity Red	06/02/2012 $125 Limited-Release	$150-$180
#125	Air Jordan 1 (I) Retro High KO "Barcelona"		Stealth/Sunburst-University Blue-White	07/21/2012 $125 GR	$110-$130
#126	Air Jordan 1 (I) Retro High (J2K Pack)		Black/Varsity Red-White	08/04/2012 $135 GR	$140-$160

(2012) Air Jordan 1 (I) Retro

Picture:	Name:	Shoe Box:	Colorway:	Release Date/Retail Price/ Release Type	Market Value for DS (2013)
#127	Air Jordan 1 (I) Retro High "Election Day"		Obsidian/ Sail-Gym Red	11/10/2012 $110 GR	$150-$170
#128	Air Jordan 1 (I) Retro High (QS) "Gucci"		Black/Gorge Green/Gym Red	12/01/2012 $110 Limited Release	$140-$160
#129	Air Jordan 1 (I) Retro High TXT		Gym Red/Black-Gym Red	12/31/2012 $120 GR	$90-$110

Did you know?
The first Air Jordan logo, the Winged Basketball, was conceived by a designer's drawing on a cocktail napkin.

AIR JORDAN 2 (II)

Air Jordan 2 (II)

The huge success of the Air Jordan 1 (I) motivated Nike to create the next Air Jordan line, the Air Jordan 2 (II) in 1986. This was supposedly the last Air Jordan to be designed by Peter Moore. The Air Jordan II (2)'s featured Italian leather as the design of the shoes was inspired by a 19th century woman's Italian boot. The shoes originally released in a black, red, and white colorway. During Michael's second basketball season, he was mostly seen wearing them on the court. Due to the popularity of these shoes, Air Jordans quickly gained traction.

During the 1986-1987 NBA season, Michael Jordan became the first player since Wilt Chamberlain to top 3,000 points in a single season.

(1986) Air Jordan 2 (II) Original

Picture:	Name:	Shoe Box:	Colorway:	Release Date/Retail Price/ Release Type	Market Value for DS (2013)
#130	Air Jordan 2 (II) Original		White/Red-Grey	11/1986 $100 GR	$900 +
#131	Air Jordan 2 (II) Original		White/ Black-Red	1986 $100 GR	$800 +

(1987) Air Jordan 2 (II) Original Low

Picture:	Name:	Shoe Box:	Colorway:	Release Date/Retail Price/ Release Type	Market Value for DS (2013)
#132	Air Jordan 2 (II) Original Low		White/ Black- Red	1987 N/A GR	$850 +
#133	Air Jordan 2 (II) Original Low		White/Red-Grey	1987 N/A GR	$1,200 +

(1994) Air Jordan 2 (II) Retro

Picture:	Name:	Shoe Box:	Colorway:	Release Date/Retail Price/ Release Type	Market Value for DS (2013)
#134	Air Jordan 2 (II) Retro (PR: '86)		White/Red Black	1994 $100 GR	$360-$380+

(1994) Air Jordan 2 (II) Retro Low

Picture:	Name:	Shoe Box:	Colorway:	Release Date/Retail Price/ Release Type	Market Value for DS (2013)
#135	Air Jordan 2 (II) Retro Low (PR: '87)		White/Red Black	1994 N/A GR	$250-$280+

(2004) Air Jordan 2 (II) Retro

Picture:	Name:	Shoe Box:	Colorway:	Release Date/Retail Price/ Release Type	Market Value for DS (2013)
#136	Air Jordan 2 (II) Retro Low (PR: '86, '94)		White/ Varsity Red/ Black	03/27/2004 $100 GR	$190-$220

(2004) Air Jordan 2 (II) Retro

Picture:	Name:	Shoe Box:	Colorway:	Release Date/Retail Price/ Release Type	Market Value for DS (2013)
#137	Air Jordan 2 (II) Retro "Chrome"		Black/ Chrome	04/24/2004 $110 GR	$210-$230
#138	Air Jordan 2 (II) Retro (LS) "Melo"		White/ Columbia Blue/Varsity Maize	04/24/2004 $110 Limited-Release	$230-$270

(2004) Air Jordan 2 (II) Retro Low

Picture:	Name:	Shoe Box:	Colorway:	Release Date/Retail Price/ Release Type	Market Value for DS (2013)
#139	Air Jordan 2 (II) Retro Low (PR: '87)		White/ Red	10/09/2004 $100 GR	$150-$170
#140	Air Jordan 2 (II) Retro Low		White/ University Blue/Black	12/11/2004 $100 GR	$140-$160

Fact:
The Air Jordan 2 (II) was the only pair of Jordans to be made in Italy.

(2005) Air Jordan 2 (II) Retro Low

Picture:	Name:	Shoe Box:	Colorway:	Release Date/Retail Price/ Release Type	Market Value for DS (2013)
#141	Air Jordan 2 (II) Retro Low		White/Metallic Silver-Varsity Maize	05/21/2005 $100 GR	$100-$120
#142	(W) Air Jordan 2 (II) Retro Low		White/Pink	05/21/2005 $100 GR-(W)	$80-$90

(2007) Air Jordan 2 (II) Retro

Picture:	Name:	Shoe Box:	Colorway:	Release Date/Retail Price/ Release Type	Market Value for DS (2013)
#143	Air Jordan 2 (II) Retro Doernbecher "Peacock"		Black/Pro Gold-Lucky Green	11/09/2007 $140 Limited Release	$430-$470

Did you know?
The Air Jordan 2 (II) was the first Nike shoe to not feature the swoosh branding anywhere on the sneaker.

(2008) Air Jordan 2 (II) Retro

Picture:	Name:	Shoe Box:	Colorway:	Release Date/Retail Price/ Release Type	Market Value for DS (2013)
#144	Air Jordan 2 (II) Retro (CDP) (PR: '86)		White/ Red-Grey	04/26/2008 $310 for pack Limited Release	$150-$170
#145	Air Jordan 2 (II) Retro "Eminem"		Black/ Stealth-Varsity Red	12/18/2008 $110 313 Pairs Made	$1,300+

(2010) Air Jordan 2 (II) Retro

Picture:	Name:	Shoe Box:	Colorway:	Release Date/Retail Price/ Release Type	Market Value for DS (2013)
#146	Air Jordan 2 (II) Retro 25th "Silver Anniversary"		Metallic Silver-Natural Grey	02/27/2010 $135 N/A	$135-$155
#147	Air Jordan 2 (II) Retro Premio "BIN 23"		Cinder/ Black	04/10/2010 $175 Limited Release 1,097 pairs	$720-$750+

(2010) Air Jordan 2 (II) Retro

Picture:	Name:	Shoe Box:	Colorway:	Release Date/Retail Price/Release Type	Market Value for DS (2013)
#148	Air Jordan 2 (II) Retro (PR:'86, '94, '04)		White/Black-Varsity Red	05/22/2010 $135 GR	$210-$230
#149	Air Jordan 2 (II) Retro QF		University Blue/Black-White off White	07/31/2010 $135 GR	$140-$160
#150	Air Jordan 2 (II) Retro QF		Del Sol/Black-White	11/06/2010 $135 GR	$160-$180
#151	Air Jordan 2 (II) Retro QF		Varsity Red/Black-White	11/06/2010 $135 GR	$140-$160
#152	Air Jordan 2 (II) Retro QF		Classic Green/Black-White	11/06/2010 $135 GR	$130-$150

AIR JORDAN 3 (III)

Air Jordan 3 (III)

Designed by Tinker Hatfield, the Air Jordan 3 (III) made its debut in 1988. The Air Jordan 3 (III)'s featured a visible air unit under the heel, a new Jumpman logo, and tumble leather to give it a unique luxurious look and feel.

Filmmaker and actor Spike Lee collaborated with Michael Jordan for a series of commercials to promote the Air Jordan 3 (III). In the commercials, Lee reprised his role as his "She's Gotta Have It" Character, Mars Blackmon. The "Mars & Mike" campaign became one of Nike's most successful campaigns.

(1988) Air Jordan 3 (III) Original

Picture:	Name:	Shoe Box:	Colorway:	Release Date/Retail Price/ Release Type	Market Value for DS (2013)
#153	Air Jordan 3 (III) Original "White Cement"		White/Cement Grey	1988 $100 GR	$1,200 +
#154	Air Jordan 3 (III) Original "Black Cement"		Black/Cement Grey	1988 $100 GR	$1,100 +
#155	Air Jordan 3 (III) Original "Fire Red"		White/Fire Red	1988 $100 GR	$1,300 +
#156	Air Jordan 3 (III) Original "True Blue"		White/Cement Grey-True Blue	1988 $100 GR	$1,200 +

Did you know?
Some say these were Michael's favorite shoe of the Air Jordan line. He wore them during the 1988 NBA Slam Dunk contest.

(1994) Air Jordan 3 (III) Retro

Picture:	Name:	Shoe Box:	Colorway:	Release Date/Retail Price/ Release Type	Market Value for DS (2013)
#157	Air Jordan 3 (III) Retro "White Cement" (PR: '88)		White/ Cement Grey	1994 $105 GR	$400 +
#158	Air Jordan 3 (III) Retro "Black Cement" (PR: '88)		Black/ Cement Grey	1994 $105 GR	$450 +

(2001) Air Jordan 3 (III) Retro

Picture:	Name:	Shoe Box:	Colorway:	Release Date/Retail Price/ Release Type	Market Value for DS (2013)
#159	Air Jordan 3 (III) Retro "Black Cement" (PR: '88, '94)		Black/ Cement Grey	07/14/2001 $100 GR	$380 +
#160	Air Jordan 3 (III) Retro "True Blue" (PR: '88)		White/ True Blue	11/17/2001 $100 GR	$230-$260
#161	Air Jordan 3 (III) Retro "Mocha"		White/ Dark Mocha	09/15/2001 $100 GR	$250-$270 +

(2003) Air Jordan 3 (III) Retro

Picture:	Name:	Shoe Box:	Colorway:	Release Date/Retail Price/ Release Type	Market Value for DS (2013)
#162	Air Jordan 3 (III) Retro "White Cement" (PR: '88)		White/ Cement Grey- Fire Red	04/19/2003 $100 GR	$270-$300

(2007) Air Jordan 3 (III) Retro

Picture:	Name:	Shoe Box:	Colorway:	Release Date/Retail Price/ Release Type	Market Value for DS (2013)
#163	Air Jordan 3 (III) Retro (LS) "Cool Grey"		Silver/Sport Red-Light Graphite- Orange Peel	02/24/2007 $135 Limited-Release	$230-$250
#164	Air Jordan 3 (III) Retro "White Flip"		White/Black- Metallic Silver/ Varsity Red	03/24/2007 $150 Limited-Release	$240-$260
#165	Air Jordan 3 (III) Retro "Fire Red" (PR: '88)		White/Fire Red-Cement Grey	03/24/2007 $125 GR	$230-$260

(2007) Air Jordan 3 (III) Retro

Picture:	Name:	Shoe Box:	Colorway:	Release Date/Retail Price/ Release Type	Market Value for DS (2013)
#166	(W) Air Jordan 3 (III) Retro "Harbor"		White/ Harbor Blue- Boarder Blue	03/24/2007 $125 GR- Women	$140- $160
#167	Air Jordan 3 (III) Retro (LS) "DTRT"		Brisk Blue/ Pro Gold- Radiant Green	04/14/2007 $135 Limited- Release	$300- $330
#168	Air Jordan 3 (III) Retro "Pure"		White/ Metallic Silver	05/12/2007 $125 GR	$190- $220
#169	Air Jordan 3 (III) Retro "Blackcat"		Black/Dark Charcoal/ Black	06/16/2007 $125 GR	$230- $260

Did you know?

The Air Jordan 3 (III) was the first shoe Tinker Hatfield designed when he first became the head designer for the Air Jordan line.

(2008) Air Jordan 3 (III) Retro

Picture:	Name:	Shoe Box:	Colorway:	Release Date/Retail Price/ Release Type	Market Value for DS (2013)
#170	Air Jordan 3 (III) Retro "Black Cement" (PR:'88, '94, '01)		Black/ Cement Grey-Varsity Red	10/18/2008 $310 Pack Limited-Release	$280-$310

(2009) Air Jordan 3 (III) Retro

Picture:	Name:	Shoe Box:	Colorway:	Release Date/Retail Price/ Release Type	Market Value for DS (2013)
#171	Air Jordan 3 (III) Retro "True Blue" (PR:'88, '01)		White/True Blue	08/08/2009 N/A International Release	$240-$280

Fact:
During the years 1987-1988, Michael Jordan won the Slam Dunk contest, the All Star MVP, the All-Defensive First Team, and the Defensive Player of the Year all while wearing the Air Jordan 3 (III).

(2010) Air Jordan 3 (III) Retro

Picture:	Name:	Shoe Box:	Colorway:	Release Date/Retail Price/ Release Type	Market Value for DS (2013)
#172	Air Jordan 3 (III) Retro "Anniversary"		White/ Metallic Silver Anniversary	05/12/2010 $125 GR	$170-$190
#173	Air Jordan 3 (III) Retro Doernbecher		Varsity Red/ Black-Metallic Silver	12/4/2010 $160 Limited Release	$630+

(2011) Air Jordan 3 (III) Retro

Picture:	Name:	Shoe Box:	Colorway:	Release Date/Retail Price/ Release Type	Market Value for DS (2013)
#174	Air Jordan 3 (III) Retro) "White Cement" (PR:'88,'94, '03)		White/ Cement Grey	01/19/2011 $150 GR	$220-$240
#175	Air Jordan 3 (III) Retro "BHM"		Black/ Metallic Gold	02/26/2011 $175 Limited Release	$200-$220

(2011) Air Jordan 3 (III) Retro

Picture:	Name:	Shoe Box:	Colorway:	Release Date/Retail Price/ Release Type	Market Value for DS (2013)
#176	Air Jordan 3 (III) Retro "Black Cement" (PR: '88, '94, '01, '08)		Black/ Varsity Red/ Cement Grey	11/25/2011 $150 GR	$240-$270
#177	Air Jordan 3 (III) Retro "True Blue" (PR: '88, '01, '09)		White/True Blue	06/19/2011 $150 GR	$230-$250
#178	Air Jordan 3 (III) Retro "Stealth"		Stealth/ Varsity Red-Light Graphite-Black	09/03/2011 $150 GR	$150-$160
#179	Air Jordan 3 (III) Retro "Black Flip"		Black/ Metallic Silver	12/03/2011 $175 Limited-Release	$180-$200
#180	(GS) Air Jordan 3 (III) Retro		Cool Grey/Blue Glow	12/03/2011 $110 GS release	$100-$110

Did you know?
The Air Jordan 3 (III) was the first Air Jordan to feature the Jumpman logo.

AIR JORDAN 4 (IV)

Air Jordan 4 (IV)

The Air Jordan 4 (IV) was designed by Tinker Hatfield, and released in 1989. The Air Jordan 4 (IV) was the first line of Jordans to include an over-molded mesh. In addition to being featured in Spike Lee's film, "Do the Right Thing", the 4's were the first of the Air Jordan line to be released on a global market.

A notable moment that made the Air Jordan 4 (IV) famous was when Michael Jordan made "The Shot" in Game 5 of the 1989 NBA First Round Playoffs between the Chicago Bulls and the Cleveland Cavaliers.

(1989) Air Jordan 4 (IV) Original

Picture:	Name:	Shoe Box:	Colorway:	Release Date/Retail Price/ Release Type	Market Value for DS (2013)
#181	Air Jordan 4 (IV) Original "White Cement"		White/Black-Cement Grey	02/1989 $110 GR	$1,000 +
#182	Air Jordan 4 (IV) Original "Bred"		Black/ Cement Grey	02/1989 $110 GR	$950 +
#183	Air Jordan 4 (IV) Original "Military"		Off White-Military Blue	Summer 1989 $110 GR	$1,000 +
#184	Air Jordan 4 (IV) Original "Fire Red"		White/Red-Black	11/1989 $110 GR	$950 +

Did you know?

In honor of "The Shot", Jordan Brand released the Air Jordan 4 (IV) using the colors of the 1989 Cleveland Cavaliers and nicknamed them the Air Jordan 4 (IV) "Cavs".

(1999) Air Jordan 4 (IV) Retro

Picture:	Name:	Shoe Box:	Colorway:	Release Date/Retail Price/ Release Type	Market Value for DS (2013)
#185	Air Jordan 4 (IV) Retro "Bred" (PR: '89)		Black/Red/ Cement Grey	05/05/1999 $100 GR	$430-$460
#186	Air Jordan 4 (IV) Retro "Cement" (PR: '89)		White/Black	06/02/1999 $100 GR	$500-$550
#187	Air Jordan 4 (IV) Retro "Columbia"		White/ Columbia Blue/ Midnight Navy	1999 $100 GR	$270-$300
#188	Air Jordan 4 (IV) Retro "Oreo"		Black/Black/ Cool Grey	11/1999 $100 GR	$360-$400+

Did you know?

A unique feature to the Air Jordan 4 (IV)'s is the upside down label on the tongue which is based on 1980's phenomenon of wearing your tongue down over the shoes making the label the right way around.

(2000) Air Jordan 4 (IV) Retro

Picture:	Name:	Shoe Box:	Colorway:	Release Date/Retail Price/ Release Type	Market Value for DS (2013)
#189	Air Jordan 4 (IV) Retro		White/ White/ Chrome	04/01/2000 $100 GR	$250-$280

(2004) Air Jordan 4 (IV) Retro

Picture:	Name:	Shoe Box:	Colorway:	Release Date/Retail Price/ Release Type	Market Value for DS (2013)
#190	Air Jordan 4 (IV) Retro		White/ Chrome/ Classic Green	07/24/2004 $100 GR	$210-$230
#191	Air Jordan 4 (IV) Retro Retro "Cool Grey"		Cool Grey/ Chrome/ Dark Charcoal/ Varsity Maize	09/25/2004 $100 GR	$330-$370

Quote:

"I've missed more than 9,000 shots in my career. I've lost almost 300 games. 26 times, I've been trusted to take the game winning shot and missed. I've failed over and over and over again in my life. And that is why I succeed."

-Michael Jordan

(2005) Air Jordan 4 (IV) Retro L.E.

Picture:	Name:	Shoe Box:	Colorway:	Release Date/Retail Price/ Release Type	Market Value for DS (2013)
#192	Air Jordan 4 (IV) Retro "Black Laser"		White/ Fire-Red/ Black	08/20/2005 $175 Limited-Release	$600 +
#193	Air Jordan 4 (IV) Retro "Fire Red" Laser Edition (PR: '89)		Black Varsity Red/ Medium Grey	05/14/2005 $200 Limited-Release	$390-$420

(2005) Air Jordan 4 (IV) Retro L.E.

Picture:	Name:	Shoe Box:	Colorway:	Release Date/Retail Price/ Release Type	Market Value for DS (2013)
#194	Air Jordan 4 (IV) Retro "Unde-feated"		Olive-Oiled Suede-Flight Satin	06/23/2005 N/A Auction Limited	$4,000 +
#195	Air Jordan 4 (IV) Retro Eminem "Encore"		Blue/Black Lt Grey	2005 N/A Limited-Release	$4,500 +

(2006) Air Jordan 4 (IV) Retro L.E.

Picture:	Name:	Shoe Box:	Colorway:	Release Date/Retail Price/ Release Type	Market Value for DS (2013)
#196	Air Jordan 4 (IV) Retro (LS) "Thunder"		Black/Tour Yellow Thunder	08/23/2006 $500 Limited-Release	$340-$380
#197	Air Jordan 4 (IV) Retro (LS) "Lightning"		Tour Yellow/Dark Blue-Grey-White	08/25/2006 $250 Limited-Release	$540-$570+

(2006) Air Jordan 4 (IV) Retro

Picture:	Name:	Shoe Box:	Colorway:	Release Date/Retail Price/ Release Type	Market Value for DS (2013)
#198	Air Jordan 4 (IV) Retro "Black Cat"		Black/Black/Light Graphite	05/20/2006 $115 GR	$250-$280
#199	Air Jordan 4 (IV) Retro "Pure"		White/Metallic Silver	05/20/2006 $115 GR	$170-$190

(2006) Air Jordan 4 (IV) Retro

Picture:	Name:	Shoe Box:	Colorway:	Release Date/Retail Price/ Release Type	Market Value for DS (2013)
#200	Air Jordan 4 (IV) Retro (LS) "Tour Yellow"		White/Tour Yellow-Dark Blue Grey-Black	08/23/2006 $125 Limited-Release	**$310-$340**
#201	Air Jordan 4 (IV) Retro (LS) "Mist Blue"		Mist Blue/ University Blue-Gold Leaf-White	06/24/2006 $125 Limited-Release	**$260-$300**

(2006) Air Jordan 4 (IV) Retro

Picture:	Name:	Shoe Box:	Colorway:	Release Date/Retail Price/ Release Type	Market Value for DS (2013)
#202	Air Jordan 4 (IV) Retro "Fire Red-Mars" (PR: '89, '05)		White/ Varsity Red-Black	07/22/2006 $115 GR	**$220-$250**
#203	Air Jordan 4 (IV) Retro "Military" (PR: '89)		White/ Military Blue-Neutral Grey	09/09/2006 $115 GR	**$160-$180**

(2006) Air Jordan 4 (IV) Retro

Picture:	Name:	Shoe Box:	Colorway:	Release Date/Retail Price/ Release Type	Market Value for DS (2013)
 #204	(W) Air Jordan 4 (IV) Retro		White/ Boarder Blue-Light Sand	07/22/2006 $115 GR-Women	$150-$170

(2007) Air Jordan 4 (IV) Retro

Picture:	Name:	Shoe Box:	Colorway:	Release Date/Retail Price/ Release Type	Market Value for DS (2013)
 #205	Air Jordan 4 (IV) Retro Promo "Motor sport"		White/ Varsity Royal-Black	03/13/2007 N/A 16 Pairs	$8,000+

(2008) Air Jordan 4 (IV) Retro

Picture:	Name:	Shoe Box:	Colorway:	Release Date/Retail Price/ Release Type	Market Value for DS (2013)
 #206	Air Jordan 4 (IV) Retro (CDP) "Bred" (PR: '89, '99)		Black-Cement Grey/Fire Red	07/19/2008 $310 GR	$220-$240

(2010) Air Jordan 4 (IV) Retro

Picture:	Name:	Shoe Box:	Colorway:	Release Date/Retail Price/ Release Type	Market Value for DS (2013)
#207	Air Jordan 4 (IV) Retro "Anniversary"		White/Metallic Silver	03/27/2010 $150 Limited-Release	$175-$200

(2011) Air Jordan 4 (IV) Retro

Picture:	Name:	Shoe Box:	Colorway:	Release Date/Retail Price/ Release Type	Market Value for DS (2013)
#208	Air Jordan 4 (IV) Retro Doernbecher		Black/Old Royal/Electric Blue/Electric Green/White	11/08/2011 $175 Limited Release	$600+

(2012) Air Jordan 4 (IV) Retro

Picture:	Name:	Shoe Box:	Colorway:	Release Date/Retail Price/ Release Type	Market Value for DS (2013)
#209	Air Jordan 4 (IV) Retro "Cement" (PR: '89, '99)		White/Black-Tech Grey	02/18/2012 $160 GR	$250-$280

(2012) Air Jordan 4 (IV) Retro

Picture:	Name:	Shoe Box:	Colorway:	Release Date/Retail Price/ Release Type	Market Value for DS (2013)
#210	Air Jordan 4 (IV) Retro (QS) "Cavs"		Black/ Orange Blaze-Old Royal	05/12/2012 $160 GR	$240-$270
#211	(GS) Air Jordan 4 (IV) Retro		White/ Ultraviolet-Black	04/14/2012 $110 GS release	$170-$190
#212	Air Jordan 4 (IV) Retro "Military" (PR: '06, '89)		White/ Neutral Grey-Military Blue	06/09/2012 $160 GR	$180-$200

(2012) Air Jordan 4 (IV) Retro

Picture:	Name:	Shoe Box:	Colorway:	Release Date/Retail Price/ Release Type	Market Value for DS (2013)
#213	Air Jordan 4 (IV) Retro "Fire Red" (PR: '89, '04, '06)		White/ Varsity Red-Black	08/04/2012 $160 GR	$180-$210

(2012) Air Jordan 4 (IV) Retro

Picture:	Name:	Shoe Box:	Colorway:	Release Date/Retail Price/ Release Type	Market Value for DS (2013)
#214	Air Jordan 4 (IV) Retro "Bred" (PR: '88, '99, 08)		Black/ Cement Grey-Fire Red	11/23/2012 $160 GR	**$220-$260**
#215	Air Jordan 4 (IV) Retro "Thunder" (PR: '06)		Black/Tour Yellow Thunder	12/22/2012 $160 Limited Release	**$200-$230**

Quote:

"Even when I'm old and grey, I won't be able to play it, but I'll still love the game."

-Michael Jordan

AIR JORDAN 5 (V)

Air Jordan 5 (V)

The Air Jordan 5 (V)'s were similar to the Air Jordan 4 (IV)'s that released the previous year. Innovative Nike shoe designer Tinker Hatfield added clear rubber soles giving them an icy appearance. This was the first Air Jordan shoe to come out during the amazing ride of the Chicago Bulls during the 1990's.

The shoe's design imitated World War II fighter planes. The soles creatively incorporated a shark teeth design similar to those painted on by WWII American fighter pilots to intimidate their enemies.

(1990) Air Jordan 5 (V) Original

Picture:	Name:	Shoe Box:	Colorway:	Release Date/Retail Price/ Release Type	Market Value for DS (2013)
#216	Air Jordan 5 (V) Original "Fire Red"		White/Black-Fire Red	02/1990 $124.99 GR	$600 +
#217	Air Jordan 5 (V) Original "Metallic"		Black/Black-Metallic Silver	02/1990 $124.99 GR	$600 +
#218	Air Jordan 5 (V) Original "Grape"		White/Grape Ice-New Emerald	1990 $124.99 GR	$750 +
#219	Air Jordan 5 (V) Original "Fire Red #23"		White/Red-Black	11/1990 $124.99 GR	$750 +

Quote:

"Some people want it to happen, some wish it would happen, and others make it happen."

-Michael Jordan

(2000) Air Jordan 5 (V) Retro

Picture:	Name:	Shoe Box:	Colorway:	Release Date/Retail Price/ Release Type	Market Value for DS (2013)
#220	Air Jordan 5 (V) Retro "Fire Red" (PR: '90)		White/Black-Fire Red	01/05/2000 $115 GR	$280-$320
#221	Air Jordan 5 (V) Retro "Metallic" (PR: '90)		Black/Black/Metallic Silver	03/15/2000 $120 GR	$300-$350
#222	Air Jordan 5 (V) Retro "Laney"		White/Varsity Royal/Varsity Maize	05/10/2000 $120 GR	$280-$320
#223	Air Jordan 5 (V) Retro		White/Metallic Silver/Black	07/01/2000 $120 GR	$260-$280

(2006) Air Jordan 5 (V) Retro

Picture:	Name:	Shoe Box:	Colorway:	Release Date/Retail Price/ Release Type	Market Value for DS (2013)
#224	Air Jordan 5 (V) Retro (LS)		Black/University Blue-White	08/19/2006 $145 Limited-Release	$250-$270

(2006) Air Jordan 5 (V) Retro

Picture:	Name:	Shoe Box:	Colorway:	Release Date/Retail Price/ Release Type	Market Value for DS (2013)
#225	Air Jordan 5 (V) Retro (LS) "Grape" (PR: '90)		White/Grape Ice-New Emerald	09/30/2006 $145 Limited-Release	**$350-$380**
#226	Air Jordan 5 (V) Retro "Stealth"		White/Sport Royal/ Stealth	10/21/2006 $135 GR	**$250-$280**
#227	Air Jordan 5 (V) Retro (LS) "Olive"		Army Olive/ Solar Orange-Black	11/18/2006 $145 Limited-Release	**$270-$310**
#228	Air Jordan 5 (V) Retro "Green Bean"		Silver-Green Bean-Flint Grey	09/23/2006 $135 GR	**$250-$280**
#229	Air Jordan 5 (V) Retro (LS) "Burgundy"		Deep Burgundy/ Light Graphite-Silver	12/16/2006 $145 Limited-Release	**$280-$320**

(2006) Air Jordan 5 (V) Retro

Picture:	Name:	Shoe Box:	Colorway:	Release Date/Retail Price/ Release Type	Market Value for DS (2013)
#230	Air Jordan 5 (V) Retro "Fire Red #23" (PR: '90)		White/Fire Red-Black	12/16/2006 $135 GR	$270-$300
#231	(W) Air Jordan 5 (V) Retro		White/Fire Red Sunset-Dark Cinder	09/23/2006 $135 GR-Women	$180-$220
#232	(W) Air Jordan 5 (V) Retro		Silver/Shy Pink-Stealth	10/21/2006 $135 GR-Women	$150-$170

(2007) Air Jordan 5 (V) Retro

Picture:	Name:	Shoe Box:	Colorway:	Release Date/Retail Price/ Release Type	Market Value for DS (2013)
#233	Air Jordan 5 (V) Retro (LS) "Laser"		White/Army Olive-Solar Orange-Bison	01/18/2007 $175 Limited-Release	$350-$380

(2007) Air Jordan 5 (V) Retro

Picture:	Name:	Shoe Box:	Colorway:	Release Date/Retail Price/ Release Type	Market Value for DS (2013)
 #234	Air Jordan 5 (V) Retro "Metallic" (PR: '90,'00)		Black/Metallic Silver-Fire Red	01/20/2007 $135 GR	$230-$260

(2007) Air Jordan 5 (V) Retro Low

Picture:	Name:	Shoe Box:	Colorway:	Release Date/Retail Price/ Release Type	Market Value for DS (2013)
 #235	(W) Air Jordan 5 (V) Retro Low		White/University Blue-Team Red	12/20/2006 $120 GR-Women	$110-$130
#236	(W) Air Jordan 5 (V) Retro Low		White/Black-Metallic Silver	01/20/2007 $120 GR-Women	$110-$130

Did you know?
The Air Jordan 5 (V) were the first basketball sneakers to feature 3M reflective material and the first Air Jordan to include a translucent sole.

(2008) Air Jordan 5 (V) Retro

Picture:	Name:	Shoe Box:	Colorway:	Release Date/Retail Price/ Release Type	Market Value for DS (2013)
#237	Air Jordan 5 (V) Retro (CDP) "Fire Red" (PR: '90, '00)		White/Black-Fire Red	08/23/2008 $310 Pack Limited-Release	$250-$280

(2009) Air Jordan 5 (V) Retro

Picture:	Name:	Shoe Box:	Colorway:	Release Date/Retail Price/ Release Type	Market Value for DS (2013)
#238	Air Jordan 5 (V) Retro (DMP) Raging Bulls Pack "3M"		Black/Varsity Red-White	05/30/2009 $310 Pack Limited Release	$280-$300
#239	Air Jordan 5 (V) Retro (DMP) Raging Bulls Pack "Toro"		Varsity Red/White-Black	05/30/2009 $310 Pack Limited Release	$400-$430
#240	Air Jordan 5 (V) Retro		White/Dark Cinder-Dark Army-Del Sol	06/2009 $135 Limited Release (Overseas)	$240-$270

(2011) Air Jordan 5 (V) Retro

Picture:	Name:	Shoe Box:	Colorway:	Release Date/Retail Price/ Release Type	Market Value for DS (2013)
#241	Air Jordan 5 (V) Retro Premio Bin 23		Black/Black-Metallic Silver	02/18/2011 $175 Limited-Release	$600-$700
#242	Air Jordan 5 (V) Retro "Wolf Grey"		Light Graphite/White-Wolf Grey	05/14/2011 $150 GR	$220-$260
#243	Air Jordan 5 (V) Retro (T23) "Tokyo23"		Varsity-Maize/Anthracite-Wolf Grey-Black	04/29/2011 $206 Limited-Release in Tokyo	$1000+
#244	Air Jordan 5 (V) Retro "Olympic"		White/Varsity Red-Mid Navy	07/02/2011 $150 Limited Release	$140-$160
#245	Air Jordan 5 (V) Retro "Metallic" (PR: '90, '00, '07)		Black/Varsity Red-Metallic Silver	08/20/2011 $150 GR	$230-$260

(2011) Air Jordan 5 (V) Retro

Picture:	Name:	Shoe Box:	Colorway:	Release Date/Retail Price/ Release Type	Market Value for DS (2013)
#246	Air Jordan 5 (V) Retro "Quai 54"		White/ Radiant Green/ Black/ Metallic Silver 3M	06/02/2011 $150 Limited Release in Europe	$350 +
#247	Air Jordan 5 (V) Retro "Black Quai 54"		Black/ Radiant Green	07/02/2011 N/A Limited-Release	$1,200 +

Fact

The Air Jordan 5 (V)'s was the last Air Jordan model released before Michael Jordan would go on to win his first NBA Championship with the Chicago Bulls in 1991.

Air Jordan 6 (VI)

Air Jordan 6 (VI)

Nike released the Air Jordan 6 (VI)'s in 1991. The shoes released during the first of two three-peat championships Michael Jordan would lead the Chicago Bulls to in the 1990's.

Michael Jordan had additional control over the design of the Air Jordan 6 (VI). His recommendations included reinforced toe protectors and a molded heel to protect Jordan from Achilles Heel injuries.

Due to Michael experiencing trouble while putting on previous Jordans, Tinker Hatfield added two holes to the top of the tongue to allow MJ to quickly put the shoes on before a game. Hatfield also improved the clear rubber sole he created for the previous version by producing better traction of the soles on the court.

(1990) Air Jordan 6 (VI) Original

Picture:	Name:	Shoe Box:	Colorway:	Release Date/Retail Price/ Release Type	Market Value for DS (2013)
#248	Air Jordan 6 (VI) Original "White Infrared"		White/Deep Infra Red	02/1990 $125 GR	$1,000 +

(1991) Air Jordan 6 (VI) Original

Picture:	Name:	Shoe Box:	Colorway:	Release Date/Retail Price/ Release Type	Market Value for DS (2013)
#249	Air Jordan 6 (VI) Original "Black Infrared"		Black/Deep Infra Red	02/1991 $125 GR	$900 +
#250	Air Jordan 6 (VI) Original "Maroon"		White/ Maroon	1991 $125 GR	$850 +
#251	Air Jordan 6 (VI) Original "Sport Blue"		White/ Sport Blue/ Black	1991 $125 GR	$900 +

(1991) Air Jordan 6 (VI) Original

Picture:	Name:	Shoe Box:	Colorway:	Release Date/Retail Price/ Release Type	Market Value for DS (2013)
#252	Air Jordan 6 (VI) Original "Carmine"		White/Carmine	11/1991 $125 GR	$1,200+

(2000) Air Jordan 6 (VI) Retro

Picture:	Name:	Shoe Box:	Colorway:	Release Date/Retail Price/ Release Type	Market Value for DS (2013)
#253	Air Jordan 6 (VI) Retro "Black Infrared" (PR: '91)		Black/Deep Infra Red	08/23/2000 $120 GR	$530-$560
#254	Air Jordan 6 (VI) Retro "Midnight Navy"		White/Midnight Navy	10/04/2000 $120 GR	$300-$330
#255	Air Jordan 6 (VI) Retro "Olympic"		Midnight Navy/Varsity Red/White	09/15/2000 $120 Limited Release	$300-$350

Fun Fact
Jeffrey is Michael Jordan's middle name.

(2002) Air Jordan 6 (VI) Retro Low

Picture:	Name:	Shoe Box:	Colorway:	Release Date/Retail Price/ Release Type	Market Value for DS (2013)
#256	Air Jordan 6 (VI) Retro Low		Black/ Metallic Silver	04/27/2002 $105 GR	$250-$280
#257	Air Jordan 6 (VI) Retro Low		White/ University Blue	04/27/2002 $105 GR	$180-$220
#258	(W) Air Jordan 6 (VI) Retro Low		White/Coral Rose	04/27/2002 $105 GR-Women	$220-$250

(2006) Air Jordan 6 (VI) Retro

Picture:	Name:	Shoe Box:	Colorway:	Release Date/Retail Price/ Release Type	Market Value for DS (2013)
#259	Air Jordan 6 (VI) Retro (DMP)		Black/ Metallic Gold	01/28/06 $296 Package Limited-Release	$470-$500

(2008) Air Jordan 6 (VI) Retro

Picture:	Name:	Shoe Box:	Colorway:	Release Date/Retail Price/ Release Type	Market Value for DS (2013)
#260	Air Jordan 6 (VI) Retro (CDP) "Carmine" "PR: '91"		White/ Carmine-Black	05/24/2008 $310 Pack Limited Release	$430-$460
#261	Air Jordan 6 (VI) Retro "Beijing Olympic"		White/ Varsity Red-Green Bean-New Blue	06/07/2008 $150 GR	$230-$260

(2009) Air Jordan 6 (VI) Retro

Picture:	Name:	Shoe Box:	Colorway:	Release Date/Retail Price/ Release Type	Market Value for DS (2013)
#262	Air Jordan 6 (VI) Retro Doeren-becher		Midnight Navy/White-Varsity-Red Metallic	11/14/2009 $165 Limited-Release	$650 +

Did you know?
Michael Jordan won his first championship wearing the Air Jordan 6 (VI) in 1991.

(2010) Air Jordan 6 (VI) Retro

Picture:	Name:	Shoe Box:	Colorway:	Release Date/Retail Price/ Release Type	Market Value for DS (2013)
#263	Air Jordan 6 (VI) Retro "Black Varsity Red" (PR: '91,'10)		Black/ Varsity Red	01/16/2010 $150 GR	$330-$370
#264	Air Jordan 6 (VI) Retro "Motor-sport"		White/Black	03/06/2010 $175 Limited-Release	$240-$280
#265	Air Jordan 6 (VI) Retro "Oreo"		White/Black-Speckle	03/20/2010 $150 GR	$230-$260

(2010) Air Jordan 6 (VI) Retro

Picture:	Name:	Shoe Box:	Colorway:	Release Date/Retail Price/ Release Type	Market Value for DS (2013)
#266	Air Jordan 6 (VI) Retro "Piston"		Black/ Varsity Red-True Blue-Light Graphite	04/07/2010 $150 GR	$160-$190

(2010) Air Jordan 6 (VI) Retro

Picture:	Name:	Shoe Box:	Colorway:	Release Date/Retail Price/ Release Type	Market Value for DS (2013)
#267	(GS) Air Jordan 6 (VI) Retro		White/Pink Flash-Volt-Marine Blue	04/2006 $105 GS release	$100-$120
#268	Air Jordan 6 (VI) Retro "Laker"		Black/Varsity Purple-White-Varsity Maize	05/15/2011 $150 GR	$240-$260
#269	Air Jordan 6 (VI) Retro (PR: '90, '10)		White/Varsity Red-Black	06/12/2010 $150 GR	$230-$270
#270	Air Jordan 6 (VI) Retro "Black Infrared" (PR: '91,'10)		Black/Black Infra-Red	06/19/2010 $310 For Pack Limited Release	$340-$380
#271	Air Jordan 6 (VI) Retro "White Infrared" (PR: '90,'10)		White/Infra-Red-Black	06/19/2010 $310 For Pack Limited Release	$240-$270

(2012) Air Jordan 6 (VI) Retro

Picture:	Name:	Shoe Box:	Colorway:	Release Date/Retail Price/ Release Type	Market Value for DS (2013)
#272	Air Jordan 6 (VI) Retro "Olympic" (PR: '00)		White/ Midnight Navy-Varsity Red	07/07/2012 $160 GR	$190-$230
#273	Air Jordan 6 (VI) Retro (GMP) "Olympic Pack"		White/ Metallic Gold	08/18/2012 $350 Limited-Release	$220-$240
#274	(GS) Air Jordan 6 (VI) Retro		Black/Pink Flash-Marina Blue	09/01/2012 $110 GS release	$120-$130

Quote:

"I never look at the consequences of missing a big shot…when you think of the consequences you always think of a negative result."

-Michael Jordan

Air Jordan 7 (VII)

Air Jordan 7 (VII)

After the success of the Air Jordan 6 (VI)'s in 1991, Nike revealed the Air Jordan 7 (VII) in 1992. Nike added some features from a number of their other Nike shoes including Huarache technology, the prevalent change made to the Air Jordan 7 (VII)'s. Tinker Hatfield also added a neoprene sockliner, which helped to secure Michael's foot within the shoe.

As part of the Dream Team, Michael Jordan was a core member of the first group of NBA professionals to play in the Olympics. He wore the number nine on his jersey during the Olympics and this was first time Michael Jordan wore a different number, other than 23, since he started playing basketball at Laney High School.

(1991) Air Jordan 7 (VII) Original

Picture:	Name:	Shoe Box:	Colorway:	Release Date/Retail Price/Release Type	Market Value for DS (2013)
#275	Air Jordan 7 (VII) Original "Hare"		White/Light-Silver True Red	02/1991 $125 GR	$475 +

(1992) Air Jordan 7 (VII) Original

Picture:	Name:	Shoe Box:	Colorway:	Release Date/Retail Price/Release Type	Market Value for DS (2013)
#276	Air Jordan 7 (VII) Original "Bordeaux"		Black/Light Graphite-Bordeaux	02/1992 $125 GR	$500 +
#277	Air Jordan 7 (VII) Original "Raptor"		Black/Dark Charcoal-True Red	04/1992 $125 GR	$330 +
#278	Air Jordan 7 (VII) Original "Olympic"		White/Midnight Navy/True Red	1992 $125 GR	$500 +

(1992) Air Jordan 7 (VII) Original

Picture:	Name:	Shoe Box:	Colorway:	Release Date/Retail Price/ Release Type	Market Value for DS (2013)
#279	Air Jordan 7 (VII) Original "Cardinal"		White/Black Cardinal-Red/Bronze	11/1992 $125 GR	$280-$330

(2002) Air Jordan 7 (VII) Retro

Picture:	Name:	Shoe Box:	Colorway:	Release Date/Retail Price/ Release Type	Market Value for DS (2013)
#280	Air Jordan 7 (VII) Retro "Raptor" (PR: '92)		Black/Dark Charcoal/ True Red	12/14/2002 $125 GR	$220-$260
#281	Air Jordan 7 (VII) Retro "French Blue"		White/ French Blue/ Flint Grey	12/14/2002 $125 GR	$250-$280

Did you know?

Nike made an Olympic edition of the Air Jordan 7 (VII) especially for Michael Jordan to wear to the Barcelona Olympics. Instead of the number 23 on the back of the Air Jordan 7 (VII), the number 9 was replaced to represent Michael Jordan's Olympic jersey number.

(2004) Air Jordan 7 (VII) Retro

Picture:	Name:	Shoe Box:	Colorway:	Release Date/Retail Price/ Release Type	Market Value for DS (2013)
#282	Air Jordan 7 (VII) Retro "Olympic" (PR: '92)		White/Metallic Gold/Midnight Navy/True Red	08/21/2004 $125 GR	$240-$260

(2006) Air Jordan 7 (VII) Retro

Picture:	Name:	Shoe Box:	Colorway:	Release Date/Retail Price/ Release Type	Market Value for DS (2013)
#283	Air Jordan 7 (VII) Retro "Pacific Blue"		Pearl White/Bright Ceramic/Pacific Blue	04/15/2006 $135 GR	$230-$250
#284	Air Jordan 7 (VII) Retro "Cardinal" (PR: '92)		White/Black Cardinal-Red/Bronze	04/22/2006 $135 GR	$190-$220
#285	Air Jordan 7 (VII) Retro "Flint"		White/Varsity Purple/Flint-Grey	04/22/2006 $135 GR	$280-$310

(2006) Air Jordan 7 (VII) Retro

Picture:	Name:	Shoe Box:	Colorway:	Release Date/Retail Price/ Release Type	Market Value for DS (2013)
#286	Air Jordan 7 (VII) Retro (LS) "Chambray"		Black/ Chambray/ Light Graphite	02/25/2006 $135 Limited-Release	$190-$220
#287	(W) Air Jordan 7 (VII) Retro		White/ Varsity-Maize-Black	05/27/2006 $135 GR-Women	$130-$160
#288	Air Jordan 7 (VII) Retro "Citrus"		Black-Citrus-Varsity Red	06/28/2006 $135 GR	$250-$280

(2008) Air Jordan 7 (VII) Retro

Picture:	Name:	Shoe Box:	Colorway:	Release Date/Retail Price/ Release Type	Market Value for DS (2013)
#289	Air Jordan 7 (VII) Retro (CDP) "Hare" (PR: '92)		White/Light Graphite-True Red	06/21/2008 $310 For Pack Limited Release	$290-$330

(2008) Air Jordan 7 (VII) Retro

Picture:	Name:	Shoe Box:	Colorway:	Release Date/Retail Price/Release Type	Market Value for DS (2013)
#290	Air Jordan 7 (VII) Retro "Miro Olympic"		White/Sport Red-Black-Metallic Gold	07/03/2008 $175 Limited Release (not released in US)	$700+

(2009) Air Jordan 7 (VII) Retro

Picture:	Name:	Shoe Box:	Colorway:	Release Date/Retail Price/Release Type	Market Value for DS (2013)
#291	Air Jordan 7 (VII) Retro (DMP) "Raptor" (PR: '92, '02)		Black/Dark Charcoal-True Red	08/22/2009 $310 Limited-Release	$240-$270
#292	Air Jordan 7 (VII) Retro (DMP) "Magic"		White/Varsity Royal-Black	08/22/2009 $310 Limited-Release	$220-$240

Did you know?
The Air Jordan 7 (VII) was worn by Michael Jordan during the 1991-1992 season.

(2010) Air Jordan 7 (VII) Retro

Picture:	Name:	Shoe Box:	Colorway:	Release Date/Retail Price/ Release Type	Market Value for DS (2013)
#293	Air Jordan 7 (VII) Retro FTLOTG "Olympic" (PR: '92, '02)		White/Metallic Gold-True Red-Midnight Navy	08/13/2010 $150 GR	$200-$220
#294	Air Jordan 7 (VII) Retro Premio "BIN23"		White/Del Sol/Black/Challenge Red	12/26/10 $175 Limited-Release	$750-$780+

(2011) Air Jordan 7 (VII) Retro

Picture:	Name:	Shoe Box:	Colorway:	Release Date/Retail Price/ Release Type	Market Value for DS (2013)
#295	Air Jordan 7 (VII) Retro "Orion"		White/Orion Blue-Black-Infrared	03/26/2011 $150 GR	$170-$190
#296	Air Jordan 7 (VII) Retro "Bordeaux" (PR: '92)		Black/Light Graphite-Bordeaux	04/19/2011 $150 GR	$250-$280

(2011) Air Jordan 7 (VII) Retro

Picture:	Name:	Shoe Box:	Colorway:	Release Date/Retail Price/ Release Type	Market Value for DS (2013)
 #297	Air Jordan 7 (VII) Retro (YOTR) "Year of the Rabbit"		Light Silver/ Metallic Gold-True Red-White	05/07/2011 $160 Limited Release	$310-$350

(2012) Air Jordan 7 (VII) Retro

Picture:	Name:	Shoe Box:	Colorway:	Release Date/Retail Price/ Release Type	Market Value for DS (2013)
 #298	Air Jordan 7 (VII) Retro "Olympic" (PR: '94, '04,'10)		White/ Metallic Gold – Midnight Navy/True Red	07/21/2012 $160 GR	$220-$240
#299	Air Jordan 7 (VII) Retro (J2K Pack) "Filbert"		Filbert/ Natural-Obsidian-White	08/04/2012 $175 Limited-Release	$260-$280
#300	Air Jordan 7 (VII) Retro (J2K Pack) "J2K"		Obsidian/ Natural-Filbert-White	08/04/2012 $175 Limited-Release	$280-$300

(2012) Air Jordan 7 (VII) Retro

Picture:	Name:	Shoe Box:	Colorway:	Release Date/Retail Price/ Release Type	Market Value for DS (2013)
#301	(GS) Air Jordan 7 (VII) Retro		White/ Fireberry-Black-Night Blue	08/11/2012 $110 GS release	$140-$160
#302	Air Jordan 7 (VII) Retro (GMP) "Olympic Pack"		Black/Gold	08/18/2012 $350 Limited Release	$240-$270
#303	Air Jordan 7 (VII) Retro "Raptor" (PR:'92,'02, '09)		Black/Dark Charcoal-True Red	09/1/2012 $160 GR	$200-$230

Quote:

"My attitude is that if you push me towards something that you think is a weakness, then I will turn that perceived weakness into a strength."

-Michael Jordan

Air Jordan 8 (VIII)

Air Jordan 8 (VIII)

While previous models of the Air Jordan were created to reduce the weight of the shoe, the Air Jordan 8 (VIII) was the heaviest in the series at the time. The benefit of this heavier shoe was advanced ankle support and traction, however, there was a downside. Those with wider feet found the Air Jordan 8 (VIII)'s difficult to put on.

Tinker Hatfield also believe that this shoe did not need the Nike symbol to succeed. He correctly believed that MJ could carry the brand for the first time.

The pattern of the 8's differed greatly from previous versions. The Air Jordan 8 (VIII) had a stitched tongue with the Jumpman logo, and a mesh of colorful patterns on the sole and sides.

(1993) Air Jordan 8 (VIII) Original

Picture:	Name:	Shoe Box:	Colorway:	Release Date/Retail Price/ Release Type	Market Value for DS (2013)
#304	Air Jordan 8 (VIII) Original "Aqua"		Black/ Concord/ Aqua Tone	02/1993 $125 GR	$550+
#305	Air Jordan 8 (VIII) Original "Bugs Bunny"		White/Black True Red	02/1993 $135 GR	$350+
#306	Air Jordan 8 (VIII) Original "Playoff"		Black/True-Red	04/1993 $125 GR	$350+

(2003) Air Jordan 8 (VIII) Retro

Picture:	Name:	Shoe Box:	Colorway:	Release Date/Retail Price/ Release Type	Market Value for DS (2013)
#307	Air Jordan 8 (VIII) Retro "Bugs Bunny" (PR: '93)		White/Black True Red	03/01/2003 $135 GR	$260-$290

(2003) Air Jordan 8 (VIII) Retro

Picture:	Name:	Shoe Box:	Colorway:	Release Date/Retail Price/Release Type	Market Value for DS (2013)
#308	Air Jordan 8 (VIII) Retro "Black Chrome"		Black / Chrome	05/03/2003 $135 GR	$260-$280

(2003) Air Jordan 8 (VIII) Retro Low

Picture:	Name:	Shoe Box:	Colorway:	Release Date/Retail Price/Release Type	Market Value for DS (2013)
#309	Air Jordan 8 (VIII) Retro Low		White/Chrome	06/21/2003 $110 GR	$150-$170
#310	Air Jordan 8 (VIII) Retro Low "Playoffs"		Black/True Red/Del Sol	08/23/2003 $110 GR	$180-$200

Fact

When the Air Jordan 8 (VIII) was released in 1992-1993, the Chicago Bulls won their third consecutive NBA title, Michael Jordan received his seventh straight scoring title, and reached a milestone in his NBA career scoring his 20,000th point.

(2007) Air Jordan 8 (VIII) Retro

Picture:	Name:	Shoe Box:	Colorway:	Release Date/Retail Price/ Release Type	Market Value for DS (2013)
#311	Air Jordan 8 (VIII) Retro "Aqua" (PR: '93)		Black/Bright Concord/ Aquatone	09/22/2007 $140 GR	$340-$360
#312	(W) Air Jordan 8 (VIII) Retro "White Aqua"		White/ Varsity Red-Bright Concord-Aqua Tone	09/22/2007 $140 GR-Women	$180-$210
#313	Air Jordan 8 (VIII) Retro (LS) "Peapod"		Midnight Navy/Orange Blaze/Silver	09/29/2007 $150 Limited-Release	$220-$250
#314	(W) Air Jordan 8 (VIII) Retro		Ice Blue/Orange Blaze-Silver	10/20/2007 $140 GR	$180-$200
#315	Air Jordan 8 (VIII) Retro "Stealth"		White/ Stealth/ Orange Blaze/Silver	10/20/2007 $140 GR	$220-$240

(2007) Air Jordan 8 (VIII) Retro

Picture:	Name:	Shoe Box:	Colorway:	Release Date/Retail Price/ Release Type	Market Value for DS (2013)
#316	Air Jordan 8 (VIII) Retro (LS) "Black Toes"		White/ Anthracite/ Dark Orange	11/17/2007 $150 Limited-Release	$190-$210
#317	Air Jordan 8 (VIII) Retro "Playoff" (PR: '93)		Black/ Varsity Red/White	12/22/2007 $140 GR	$260-$280

(2007) Air Jordan 8 (VIII) Retro Low

Picture:	Name:	Shoe Box:	Colorway:	Release Date/Retail Price/ Release Type	Market Value for DS (2013)
#318	(W) Air Jordan 8 (VIII) Retro Low		Dark Cinder/ Champagne/ Sail	12/22/2007 $110 GR-Women	$70-80
#319	(W) Air Jordan 8 (VIII) Retro Low		Black/Real Pine-White	12/22/2007 $110 GR-Women	$70-80

(2008) Air Jordan 8 (VIII) Retro

Picture:	Name:	Shoe Box:	Colorway:	Release Date/Retail Price/ Release Type	Market Value for DS (2013)
#320	Air Jordan 8 (VIII) Retro P.E. "Sugar Ray Allen"		Black/ Stealth-Clover	02/13/2008 $140 P.E. Limited to 24 Pairs	$2,500-$3,000
#321	Air Jordan 8 (VIII) Retro P.E. "Q-Rich"		White/Blue Ribbon -Orange Flash	02/13/2008 $140 P.E. Release-Avaliable	$750 +
#322	Air Jordan 8 (VIII) Retro (CDP) "Bugs Bunny" (PR: '93,'03)		White/Black True Red	11/15/2008 $310 Pack GR	$240-$270

Fact

With over 30,000 points, 5,600 assist, 2,500 steals, and 41,000 minutes total career stats, in 2009, Michael Jordan received one of basketball's greatest honors: he was inducted into the Naismith Memorial Basketball Hall of Fame.

Air Jordan 9 (IX)

Air Jordan 9 (IX)

The Air Jordan 9 (IX)'s were distinctive for being the first shoes released after Jordan quasi-retired. (Author's note: We say quasi-retired, because he would "retire" a total of three times, before finally retiring for good in 2003.)

The shoes displayed Michael Jordan's international rising fame. Symbols like the Jumpman logo were stitched into the Japanese rising sun, along with words in different languages. These symbols reflected how MJ become a worldwide phenomenon.

A perfect example is the words listed on the bottom of the shoes. From "uhuru", which is Swahili for independence to the Spanish word "fuerza" for force, these shoes represented what Michael Jordan represented to the world.

(1993) Air Jordan 9 (IX) Original

Picture:	Name:	Shoe Box:	Colorway:	Release Date/Retail Price/ Release Type	Market Value for DS (2013)
#323	Air Jordan 9 (IX) Original "Powder"		White/Black-Black Powder	1993 $125 GR	$350 +
#324	Air Jordan 9 (IX) Original "Playoff"		White/Black True Red	11/1993 $125 GR	$350 +
#325	Air Jordan 9 (IX) Original "Olive"		Black/Light Olive/True Red	1993 $125 GR	$300 +

(1994) Air Jordan 9 (IX) Original

Picture:	Name:	Shoe Box:	Colorway:	Release Date/Retail Price/ Release Type	Market Value for DS (2013)
#326	Air Jordan 9 (IX) Original "Charcoal"		Black-Dark Charcoal-True Red	1994 $125 GR	$300 +

(2002) Air Jordan 9 (IX) Retro

Picture:	Name:	Shoe Box:	Colorway:	Release Date/Retail Price/ Release Type	Market Value for DS (2013)
#327	Air Jordan 9 (IX) Retro "Playoff" (PR: '93)		White/Black-True Red	01/12/2002 $125 GR	$190-$230
#328	Air Jordan 9 (IX) Retro "Olive" (PR: '93)		Black/Light Olive-True Red	03/09/2002 $125 GR	$250-$280
#329	Air Jordan 9 (IX) Retro "French Blue"		White/French Blue-Flint Grey	05/04/2002 $125 GR	$260-$290
#330	Air Jordan 9 (IX) Retro "Cool Grey"		Cool Grey Medium Grey White-Cool Grey	10/25/2002 $125 GR	$210-$230

(2002) Air Jordan 9 (IX) Retro Low

Picture:	Name:	Shoe Box:	Colorway:	Release Date/Retail Price/ Release Type	Market Value for DS (2013)
#331	Air Jordan 9 (IX) Retro Low		Low White/White-Chrome	07/03/2002 $115 GR	$160-$190

(2002) Air Jordan 9 (IX) Retro Low

Picture:	Name:	Shoe Box:	Colorway:	Release Date/Retail Price/ Release Type	Market Value for DS (2013)
#332	Air Jordan 9 (IX) Retro Low		White/Blue Pearl	09/21/2002 $115 GR	$170-$200

(2008) Air Jordan 9 (IX) Retro

Picture:	Name:	Shoe Box:	Colorway:	Release Date/Retail Price/ Release Type	Market Value for DS (2013)
#333	Air Jordan 9 (IX) Retro (CDP) "Playoff" (PR: '93,'02)		White/True Red – Black	03/15/2008 $310 Pack Limited Release	$190-$230

(2010) Air Jordan 9 (IX) Retro

Picture:	Name:	Shoe Box:	Colorway:	Release Date/Retail Price/ Release Type	Market Value for DS (2013)
#334	Air Jordan 9 (IX) Retro "Silver Anniversary"		White/ Metallic Silver	03/27/2010 $150 Limited-Release	$200-$230

(2010) Air Jordan 9 (IX) Retro

Picture:	Name:	Shoe Box:	Colorway:	Release Date/Retail Price/ Release Type	Market Value for DS (2013)
#335	Air Jordan 9 (IX) Retro		White/ University Blue	05/29/2010 $150 GR	$180-$220
#336	Air Jordan 9 (IX) Retro Premio BIN 23		White/ Metallic Gold	05/29/2010 and 06/5/2010 $175 Limited Release	$800-$900
#337	Air Jordan 9 (IX) Retro		Black/Citrus - White	07/03/2010 $150 GR	$170-$190
#338	Air Jordan 9 (IX) Retro "Playoff" (PR: '93,'02)		White/ Varsity-Red-Black	08/07/2010 $150 GR	$180-$220

Fun Fact

A special version of the Air Jordan 9 (IX) was made for Michael Jordan when he played baseball for the Birmingham Barons.

(2010) Air Jordan 9 (IX) Retro

Picture:	Name:	Shoe Box:	Colorway:	Release Date/Retail Price/ Release Type	Market Value for DS (2013)
#339	Air Jordan 9 (IX) Retro "FTLOTG"		University Blue/White-Black	09/07/2010 $150 N/A	$180-$210
#340	Air Jordan 9 (IX) Retro "Charcoal" (PR: '94)		Black/Dark Charcoal-True Red	09/04/2010 $150 GR	$240-$270
#341	Air Jordan 9 (IX) Retro "Quai 54"		White/Varsity-Maize	07/2010 $150 Limited to 2,000 pairs	$280+

Did you know?
The Air Jordan 9 (IX) was released in 1993 shortly after Michael Jordan shocked the world with the announcement of his retirement. Michael Jordan would not play in the Air Jordan 9 (IX) as a Chicago Bulls player.

(2012) Air Jordan 9 (IX) Retro

Picture:	Name:	Shoe Box:	Colorway:	Release Date/Retail Price/ Release Type	Market Value for DS (2013)
#342	Air Jordan 9 (IX) Retro P.E. "Oregon Ducks" Edition		Charcoal Grey/Light Graphite/ Neutral Grey	2012 N/A For University of Oregon athletes	$1,000+
#343	(GS) Air Jordan 9 (IX) Retro "Imperial Purple"		Medium Grey/White-Imperial Purple-Cool Grey	10/06/2012 $110 GS release	$110-$130
#344	Air Jordan 9 (IX) Retro "Johnny Kilroy"		Black/Metallic Platinum-Gym Red	10/06/2012 $160 Limited Release	$180-$210
#345	Air Jordan 9 (IX) Retro "Fontay Montana"		Pure Platinum/Game Royal-Mandarin	10/13/2012 $160 Limited Release	$220-$250
#346	Air Jordan 9 (IX) Retro "Bentley Ellis"		White/Dark Cayenne-University Gold	10/27/12 $160 Limited Release	$240-$260

(2012) Air Jordan 9 (IX) Retro

Picture:	Name:	Shoe Box:	Colorway:	Release Date/Retail Price/ Release Type	Market Value for DS (2013)
#347	Air Jordan 9 (IX) Retro "Calvin Bailey"		Deep Royal/ University Gold-White	11/10/2012 $160 Limited Release	$210-$240
#348	Air Jordan 9 (IX) Retro "Olive" (PR: '93,'02)		Black/Light Olive-Varsity Red	11/17/2012 $160 Limited Release	$220-$240
#349	Air Jordan 9 (IX) Retro "Slim Jenkin"		Black/Matte Silver-University Blue	11/24/2012 $160 Limited Release	$180-$210
#350	Air Jordan 9 (IX) Retro "Motorboat Jones"		Challenge Red/White/ Black	12/01/2012 $160 Limited Release	$260-$280
#351	Air Jordan 9 (IX) Retro "Cool Grey" (PR: '02)		Medium Grey/Cool Grey-White	12/15/12 $160 GR	$180-$220
#352	Air Jordan 9 (IX) Retro Doernbecher		White/ Metallic Gold-Black	11/30/2012 $175 Limited-Release	$460-$480

Air Jordan 10 (X)

Air Jordan 10 (X)

In 1995, the Air Jordan 10 (X)'s were released. Just as the Air Jordan 9 (IX) was a testament to how Michael affected the world, the Air Jordan 10 (X) reflected how Michael changed the game of basketball.

The Air Jordan 10 (X) were the first Air Jordan to feature a lightweight phylon midsole. In order to show appreciation, Tinker Hatfield and the people of Nike decided to include Michael Jordan's accomplishments during his career as an NBA player on the Air Jordan 10 (X). Michael Jordan would go on to wear this particular pair when he came out of retirement.

(1994) Air Jordan 10 (X) Original

Picture:	Name:	Shoe Box:	Colorway:	Release Date/Retail Price/ Release Type	Market Value for DS (2013)
#353	Air Jordan 10 (X) Original "Steel Grey"		White/Black-Light Steel Grey	11/1994 $125 GR	$300-$350
#354	Air Jordan 10 (X) Original "Charlotte Hornet"		White/Black Dark Powder Blue	11/1994 $125 GR	$380-$420
#355	Air Jordan 10 (X) Original "Shadow"		Black/Dark Shadow/True Red	11/1994 $125 GR	$250-$300

(1995) Air Jordan 10 (X) Original

Picture:	Name:	Shoe Box:	Colorway:	Release Date/Retail Price/ Release Type	Market Value for DS (2013)
#356	Air Jordan 10 (X) Original "Chicago"		White/Black True Red	1995 $125 Limited-Released in Chicago only	$400-$450

(1995) Air Jordan 10 (X) Original

Picture:	Name:	Shoe Box:	Colorway:	Release Date/Retail Price/ Release Type	Market Value for DS (2013)
#357	Air Jordan 10 (X) Original "Seattle"		White/Black Kelly Green/ Yellow Gold	1995 $125 Limited-Release in Seattle only	$425.00 +
#358	Air Jordan 10 (X) Original "Orlando"		White/Black Royal Blue/ Metallic Silver	1995 $125 Limited-Released in Orlando	$400.00 +
#359	Air Jordan 10 (X) Original "New York"		White/Black Royal Blue/Orange Flame	1995 $125 Limited-Released in New York	$450.00 +
#360	Air Jordan 10 (X) Original "Sacramento"		Black/Dark Concord Metallic Silver	1995 $125 Limited-Released in Sacramento	$500.00

Fact

Some of Michael Jordan's acommplishments listed on the sole of the Air Jordan 10 (X) includes his 1985 Rookie of The Year, his three Championship/MVP seasons, and the 1988 Dunk champ.

(2005) Air Jordan 10 (X) Retro

Picture:	Name:	Shoe Box:	Colorway:	Release Date/Retail Price/ Release Type	Market Value for DS (2013)
#361	Air Jordan 10 (X) Retro "Steel Grey" (PR: '94)		White/Black Steel Grey	05/07/2005 $125 GR	$250-$280
#362	Air Jordan 10 (X) Retro (LS) "Ice Blue"		White/Ice Blue	06/11/2005 $125 Limited-Release	$220-$230
#363	Air Jordan 10 (X) Retro		Black/Black	07/23/2005 $125 GR	$190-$230
#364	Air Jordan 10 (X) Retro (LS)		White/Linen-University Blue	07/23/2005 $125 Limited-Release	$250-$270

Fun Fact

In 1990, when the Chicago Bulls faced the Orlando Magis, Michael Jordan was forced to wear the Jersey number 12 instead of his usual 23 because someone stole his jersey before the game.

(2005) Air Jordan 10 (X) Retro

Picture:	Name:	Shoe Box:	Colorway:	Release Date/Retail Price/ Release Type	Market Value for DS (2013)
#365	(W) Air Jordan 10 (X) Retro		White/Ice Green-Varsity Red	07/23/2005 $125 GR-Women	$100-$110
#366	(W) Air Jordan 10 (X) Retro		White/Medium Violet-Light Graphite	09/17/2005 $125 GR-Women	$120-$140
#367	Air Jordan 10 (X) Retro		White/Varsity Red/Light Steel Grey	09/17/2005 $125 GR	$220-$250

(2008) Air Jordan 10 (X) Retro

Picture:	Name:	Shoe Box:	Colorway:	Release Date/Retail Price/ Release Type	Market Value for DS (2013)
#368	Air Jordan 10 (X) Retro (CDP) "Shadow" (PR: '94)		Black/Dark Shadow-True Red	01/19/2008 $310 Pack Limited-Release	$220-$260

(2012) Air Jordan 10 (X) Retro

Picture:	Name:	Shoe Box:	Colorway:	Release Date/Retail Price/ Release Type	Market Value for DS (2013)
#369	Air Jordan 10 (X) Retro "Chicago" (PR: '95)		White/ Varsity Red- Black	01/21/2012 $160 GR	$200- $220
#370	(GS) Air Jordan 10 (X) Retro		White/Violet Pop Cyber Black	01/21/2012 $110 GS release	$100- $120
#371	Retro Air Jordan 10 (X) Retro "Royal Stealth"		White/Old Royal- Stealth	02/11/2012 $160 GR	$190- $210
#372	Air Jordan 10 (X) Retro "Stealth"		Black/White -Stealth	03/24/2012 $160 GR	$140- $170

Did you know?

Although Michael Jordan had gone through the early stages of the design for the Air Jordan 10 (X) with Tinker Hatfield, the Air Jordan 10 (X) was the only Air Jordan at the time not approved by him.

Air Jordan 11 (XI)

Air Jordan 11 (XI)

Now that Michael Jordan was back with the Chicago Bulls for the 1995-1996 season, Tinker Hatfield wanted to create a shoe commemorative of this event.

The shiny leather shoe design, which resembled a sleek convertible with the top down, was the shoe Jordan wore during his 1995-1996 NBA season and is said to be the most popular Air Jordan model ever created.

Although the design of the shoe did not disappoint its fans, the durability and quality had the opposite reaction. The clear rubber soles easily yellowed and the patent leather was proned to crease and scratch easily.

(1995) Air Jordan 11 (XI) Original

Picture:	Name:	Shoe Box:	Colorway:	Release Date/Retail Price/ Release Type	Market Value for DS (2013)
#373	Air Jordan 11 (XI) Original "Playoff" "Bred"		Black/ VarsityRed/ White	04/1995 $125 GR	$450-$500
#374	Air Jordan 11 (XI) Original "Concord"		White/Black Dark Concord	11/1995 $125 GR	$500-$550

(1996) Air Jordan 11 (XI) Original

Picture:	Name:	Shoe Box:	Colorway:	Release Date/Retail Price/ Release Type	Market Value for DS (2013)
#375	Air Jordan 11 (XI) Original "Columbia"		White/ Columbia Blue/Black	02/1996 $125 GR	$400-$500

Fact
During the 1995-1996 season, Michael Jordan became the second person to win MVP awards for the regular season, All-Star Game and the NBA Finals all in the same season.

(1996) Air Jordan 11 (XI) Original Low

Picture:	Name:	Shoe Box:	Colorway:	Release Date/Retail Price/ Release Type	Market Value for DS (2013)
#376	Air Jordan 11 (XI) Original Low IE		Black/Dark Grey/True Red	1996 $115 GR	$220-$260
#377	Air Jordan 11 (XI) Original Low IE "Cobalt"		White/Light Grey/Cobalt	1996 $125 GR	$200-$240

(2000) Air Jordan 11 (XI) Retro

Picture:	Name:	Shoe Box:	Colorway:	Release Date/Retail Price/ Release Type	Market Value for DS (2013)
#378	Air Jordan 11 (XI) Retro "Concord" (PR: '96)		White/Black Dark Concord	10/25/2000 $125 GR	$340-$370
#379	Air Jordan 11 (XI) Retro "Space Jam"		Black/ Varsity Royal/White	12/13/2000 $125 GR	$410-$440

(2001) Air Jordan 11 (XI) Retro

Picture:	Name:	Shoe Box:	Colorway:	Release Date/Retail Price/ Release Type	Market Value for DS (2013)
#380	Air Jordan 11 (XI) Retro "Columbia" (PR: '96)		White/ Columbia Blue/Black	01/17/2001 $125 GR	$380-$410
#381	Air Jordan 11 (XI) Retro "Playoff" "Bred" (PR: '95)		Black/ Varsity Red/ White	12/22/2001 $125 GR	$370-$400
#382	Air Jordan 11 (XI) Retro "Cool Grey"		Medium Grey/White/ Cool Grey	03/03/2001 $125 GR	$280-$300

(2001) Air Jordan 11 (XI) Retro Low

Picture:	Name:	Shoe Box:	Colorway:	Release Date/Retail Price/ Release Type	Market Value for DS (2013)
#383	Air Jordan 11 (XI) Retro Low		White/ Varsity Red	04/14/2001 $115 GR	$380-$420
#384	Air Jordan 11 (XI) Retro Low		White/ Columbia Blue/	04/14/2001 $115 GR	$320-$360

(2001) Air Jordan 11 (XI) Retro Low

Picture:	Name:	Shoe Box:	Colorway:	Release Date/Retail Price/ Release Type	Market Value for DS (2013)
#385	(W) Air Jordan 11 (XI) Retro Low "Citrus"		White/Citrus	04/14/2001 $115 GR-Women	$450-$500
#386	(GS) Air Jordan 11 (XI) Retro Low		White/Hot Pink	04/14/2001 $100 GS release	$140-$180
#387	(W) Air Jordan 11 (XI) Retro Low		White/ Metallic Silver	04/14/2001 $115 GR-Women	$200-$230
#388	Air Jordan 11 (XI) Retro Low "Snake"		White/Black Navy	05/26/2001 $120 GR	$370-$400
#389	(W) Air Jordan 11 (XI) Retro Low "Snake"		White/Black -Pink	05/26/2001 $120 GR-Women	$300-$350
#390	Air Jordan 11 (XI) Retro Low "Zen Grey"		White/Light Zen Grey	06/23/2001 $115 GR	$220-$250

(2003) Air Jordan 11 (XI) Retro Low

Picture:	Name:	Shoe Box:	Colorway:	Release Date/Retail Price/ Release Type	Market Value for DS (2013)
#391	Air Jordan 11 (XI) Retro Low IE (PR: '96)		Black/Dark Grey/True Red	05/24/2003 $115 GR	$170-$190
#392	Air Jordan 11 (XI) Retro Low IE "Cobalt" (PR: '96)		White/Light Grey/Cobalt	05/24/2003 $115 GR	$150-$180

(2006) Air Jordan 11 (XI) Retro

Picture:	Name:	Shoe Box:	Colorway:	Release Date/Retail Price/ Release Type	Market Value for DS (2013)
#393	Air Jordan 11 (XI) Retro (DMP) "Concord" (PR: '96, '00)		White/ Metallic Gold-Black	01/28/2006 $296 Pack Limited Release	$380-$420

Did you know?

Michael Jordan was fined $5,000 for two games during the semifinals in 1995 for wearing the Air Jordan 11 (XI) Concords. This was in violation of the NBA dresscode. The entire Bulls team wore mainly all black shoes.

(2007) Air Jordan 11 (XI) Retro Low

Picture:	Name:	Box:	Colorway:	Release Date/Retail Price/ Release Type	Market Value for DS (2012)
#394	Air Jordan 11 (XI) Retro Low IE		Silver/Zest/ White	06/30/2007 $115 GR	$120-$160
#395	(W) Air Jordan 11 (XI) Retro Low		Black/ Metallic Gold	06/30/2007 $125 GR-Women	$70-$90
#396	Air Jordan 11 (XI) Retro Low IE		Black/Zest-White	06/30/2007 $115 GR	$170-$200
#397	(GS) Air Jordan 11 (XI) Retro Low IE		White/ Metallic Gold	07/2007 $80 GR-Youth (GS)	$80-$90
#398	Air Jordan 11 (XI) Retro Low IE (LS) "Azure"		White/ Varsity Maize/Azure	07/21/2007 $125 Limited-Release	$90-$110

(2007) Air Jordan 11 (XI) Retro Low

Picture:	Name:	Box:	Colorway:	Release Date/Retail Price/ Release Type	Market Value for DS (2012)
 #399	Air Jordan 11 (XI) Retro Low IE		White/Zest Argon Blue/Bone	08/04/2007 $115 GR	$80-$110
 #400	Air Jordan 11 (XI) Retro Low IE		Argon/Blue/ Zest/White	08/04/2007 $115 GR	$120-$150

(2008) Air Jordan 11 (XI) Retro (XI)

Picture:	Name:	Shoe Box:	Colorway:	Release Date/Retail Price/ Release Type	Market Value for DS (2013)
 #401	Air Jordan 11 (XI) Retro (CDP) "Playoff" "Bred" (PR: '95,'01)		Black/ Varsity Red-White	12/20/2008 $310 Pack Limited Release	$300-$330

Fact

Michael Jordan averaged 30.4 points during the 1995-1996 season and scored 40+ in nine games while wearing the Air Jordan 11 (XI).

(2009) Air Jordan 11 (XI) Retro (XI)

Picture:	Name:	Shoe Box:	Colorway:	Release Date/Retail Price/ Release Type	Market Value for DS (2013)
#402	Air Jordan 11 (XI) Retro (QS) "Space Jams" (PR: '00)		Black/ Varsity Royal/White	12/23/2009 $175 Limited Release	$420-$460

(2010) Air Jordan 11 (XI) Retro (XI)

Picture:	Name:	Shoe Box:	Colorway:	Release Date/Retail Price/ Release Type	Market Value for DS (2013)
#403	Air Jordan 11 (XI) Retro "Silver Anniversary"		White/ Metallic Silver	05/01/2010 $150 Limited-Release	$270-$290
#404	Air Jordan 11 (XI) Retro "Cool Grey" (PR: '01)		Medium Grey/White Cool Grey	12/23/2010 $175 GR	$300-$340

Fun Fact
The Air Jordan 11 (XI) were seen on Michael Jordan's feet in the movie "Space Jam".

(2011) Air Jordan 11 (XI) Retro Low

Picture:	Name:	Shoe Box:	Colorway:	Release Date/Retail Price/ Release Type	Market Value for DS (2013)
#405	Air Jordan 11 (XI) Retro Low IE		Black/ Varsity Red	07/16/2011 $120 GR	**$180-$210**
#406	Air Jordan 11 (XI) Retro Low IE		White/ Metallic Silver-Black	08/13/2011 $120 GR	**$160-$180**

(2011) Air Jordan 11 (XI) Retro

Picture:	Name:	Shoe Box:	Colorway:	Release Date/Retail Price/ Release Type	Market Value for DS (2013)
#407	Air Jordan 11 (XI) Retro "Concords" PR: '96, '00		White/Dark Concord-Black	12/23/2011 $180 GR	**$320-$350**

Did you know?
The Defining Moments Pack, which included the Air Jordan 6 (VI) along with the Air Jordan 11 (XI) Concord, was the first pack ever released by the Jordan brand.

(2012) Air Jordan 11 (XI) Retro Low

Picture:	Name:	Shoe Box:	Colorway:	Release Date/Retail Price/ Release Type	Market Value for DS (2013)
#408	Air Jordan 11 (XI) Retro Low		White/ Varsity Red	05/05/2012 $140 GR	$170-$200

(2012) Air Jordan 11 (XI) Retro

Picture:	Name:	Shoe Box:	Colorway:	Release Date/Retail Price/ Release Type	Market Value for DS (2013)
#409	Air Jordan 11 (XI) Retro "Playoff" "Bred" (PR: '95, '01, '08)		Black/ Varsity Red-White	12/21/2012 $185 GR	$300-$330

Quote:

"The game of basketball has been everything to me. My place of refuge, place I've always gone where I needed comfort and peace. It's been the site of intense pain and the most intense feelings of joy and satisfaction. It's a relationship that has evolved over time, given the greatest respect and love for the game."

-Michael Jordan

Air Jordan 12 (XII)

Air Jordan 12 (XII)

As Nike began to create shoes annually for the Air Jordan line, Nike ensured to improve every model with design and technology. The Air Jordan 12 (XII)'s were no exception.

This particular line paid homage to Japanese culture and woman's fashion. The design of the shoe resembles a 19th century dress boot with a Japanese flag design.

On a technical level, the Air Jordan 12 (XII) shoes were considered the most durable and sturdy shoes the line ever created. However, the shoes were heavier than previous models.

(1996) Air Jordan 12 (XII) Original

Picture:	Name:	Shoe Box:	Colorway:	Release Date/Retail Price/ Release Type	Market Value for DS (2013)
#410	Air Jordan 12 (XII) Original "Taxi"		White/Black Taxi	1996 $135 GR	$200-$250

(1997) Air Jordan 12 (XII) Original

Picture:	Name:	Shoe Box:	Colorway:	Release Date/Retail Price/ Release Type	Market Value for DS (2013)
#411	Air Jordan 12 (XII) Original "Cherry"		White/ Varsity Red/ Black	1997 $135 GR	$240-$280
#412	Air Jordan 12 (XII) Original "Obsidian"		Obsidian/ White/ French Blue	02/1997 $135 GR	$200-$230
#413	Air Jordan 12 (XII) Original "Flu Game"		Black/ Varsity Red	1997 $135 GR	$270-$300

(1997) Air Jordan 12 (XII) Original

Picture:	Name:	Shoe Box:	Colorway:	Release Date/Retail Price/ Release Type	Market Value for DS (2013)
#414	Air Jordan 12 (XII) Original "Playoff"		Black/ White/ Varsity Red/ Metallic Silver	1997 $140 GR	$220-$260

(2003) Air Jordan 12 (XII) Retro

Picture:	Name:	Shoe Box:	Colorway:	Release Date/Retail Price/ Release Type	Market Value for DS (2013)
#415	Air Jordan 12 (XII) Retro "Flu Game" (PR: '97)		Black/ Varsity Red	10/25/2003 $135 GR	$280-$320
#416	Air Jordan 12 (XII) Retro "Nubuck"		Black/ White/ University Blue	11/28/2003 $200 Limited-Release	$190-$230
#417	Air Jordan 12 (XII) Retro "Flint Grey"		White/ Flint Grey/ Silver	12/13/2003 $135 GR	$240-$260

Fact

The Air Jordan 12 (XII) would be the first Air Jordan in the Jordan Brand line.

(2004) Air Jordan 12 (XII) Retro

Picture:	Name:	Shoe Box:	Colorway:	Release Date/Retail Price/ Release Type	Market Value for DS (2013)
#418	Air Jordan 12 (XII) Retro "French Blue"		White/ French Blue/ Metallic Silver	01/10/2004 $135 GR	$280-$310
#419	Air Jordan 12 (XII) Retro "Playoff" (PR: '97)		Black/ White/ Varsity Red/ Metallic Silver	02/14/2004 $135 GR	$230-$250
#420	Air Jordan 12 (XII) Retro "Melo"		White/ University Blue/ Metallic Silver	05/15/2004 $135 GR	$220-$260

(2004) Air Jordan 12 (XII) Retro Low

Picture:	Name:	Shoe Box:	Colorway:	Release Date/Retail Price/ Release Type	Market Value for DS (2013)
#421	Air Jordan 12 (XII) Retro Low "Obsidian" (PR: '97)		Obsidian/ University Blue/ White	04/10/2004 $115 GR	$200-$240

(2004) Air Jordan 12 (XII) Retro Low

Picture:	Name:	Shoe Box:	Colorway:	Release Date/Retail Price/ Release Type	Market Value for DS (2013)
#422	Air Jordan 12 (XII) Retro Low "Taxi"		White/ Black/ Taxi	05/22/2004 $115 GR	**$180-$210**
#423	Air Jordan 12 (XII) Retro Low		White/ Real Pink Metallic Silver	06/22/2004 $115 GR	**$90-$120**

(2008) Air Jordan 12 (XII) Retro

Picture:	Name:	Shoe Box:	Colorway:	Release Date/Retail Price/ Release Type	Market Value for DS (2013)
#424	Air Jordan 12 (XII) Retro (CDP) "Taxi" (PR: '96)		Retro Black/ Black-Varsity Red	12/20/2008 $310 for Pack Limited-Release	**$230-$260**

Fun Fact

Michael Jordan routinely wore his University of North Carolina shorts under his playing shorts for good luck during NBA games.

(2009) Air Jordan 12 (XII) Retro

Picture:	Name:	Shoe Box:	Colorway:	Release Date/Retail Price/ Release Type	Market Value for DS (2013)
#425	Air Jordan 12 (XII) Retro "Nubuck" (PR: '93)		Black/White-University Blue	05/30/2009 $150 GR	$180-$220
#426	Air Jordan 12 (XII) Retro "Rising Sun"		White/Varsity Red-Black	11/21/2009 $150 Limited Release	$240-$260
#427	Air Jordan 12 (XII) Retro "Flu Game" (PR: '97,'03)		Black/Varsity Red	11/27/2009 $150 GR	$260-$290
#428	(GS) Air Jordan 12 (XII) Retro		Black-Grand Purple-Aquamarine	11/2009 $100 GS Release	$120-$140
#429	Air Jordan 12 (XII) Retro "Cherry"		White/Varsity Black	12/19/2009 $150 GR	$220-$260

(2011) Air Jordan 12 (XII) Retro Low

Picture:	Name:	Shoe Box:	Colorway:	Release Date/Retail Price/ Release Type	Market Value for DS (2013)
#430	Air Jordan 12 (XII) Retro Low "Taxi" (QS) (PR: '04)		White/ Black-Taxi	04/09/2011 $115 Limited-Release	$180-$220
#431	Air Jordan 12 (XII) Retro Low		Black/ Varsity Red	05/28/2011 $115 GR	$140-$170

(2012) Air Jordan 12 (XII) Retro

Picture:	Name:	Shoe Box:	Colorway:	Release Date/Retail Price/ Release Type	Market Value for DS (2013)
#432	Air Jordan 12 (XII) Retro "Playoff" (PR: '97,'04)		Black/ White/ Varsity Red/ Metallic Silver	04/21/2012 $160 GR	$230-$260
#433	Air Jordan 12 (XII) Retro		Cool Grey/Team Orange-White	05/19/2012 $160 GR	$210-$230

(2012) Air Jordan 12 (XII) Retro

Picture:	Name:	Shoe Box:	Colorway:	Release Date/Retail Price/ Release Type	Market Value for DS (2013)
#434	(GS) Air Jordan 12 (XII) Retro		Black/Siren Red	05/19/2012 $110 GS Release	$110-$130
#435	Air Jordan 12 (XII) Retro "Obsidian" (PR: '97)		Obsidian/White-French Blue-University Blue	06/23/2012 $160 GR	$190-$210

Did you know?
Michael Jordan's pre-game meal consisted of steak cooked medium rare, a baked potato and water or gingle ale.

Air Jordan 13 (XIII)

Air Jordan 13 (XIII)

Nike designer Tinker Hatfield knew exactly what he wanted for the Air Jordan 13 (XIII)'s. After years of watching Michael Jordan play, Hatfield saw Jordan as a panther on the court: he would prowl the field, measuring up opposing players, and strike like a panther.

Using this as an inspiration, Hatfield designed a shoe with a sole resembling a panther paw. Additionally, the shoe included a hologram with the number 23, the Jumpman logo, and a basketball. These changes made the Air Jordan 13 (XIII) a remarkabe shoe. One can envision Jordan preparing to strike and make his great shot.

(1997) Air Jordan 13 (XIII) Original

Picture:	Name:	Shoe Box:	Colorway:	Release Date/Retail Price/ Release Type	Market Value for DS (2013)
#436	Air Jordan 13 (XIII) Original "He Got Game"		White/Black True Red	11/01/1997 $150 GR	$250-$300
#437	Air Jordan 13 (XIII) Original "Playoff"		Black/True Red/White	1997 $150 GR	$260-$310

(1998) Air Jordan 13 (XIII) Original

Picture:	Name:	Shoe Box:	Colorway:	Release Date/Retail Price/ Release Type	Market Value for DS (2013)
#438	Air Jordan 13 (XIII) Original "Flint"		French Blue-University Blue-Flint Grey	02/14/1998 $150 GR	$280-$300
#439	Air Jordan 13 (XIII) Original "Bulls"		White/True Red/Black/ Pearl Grey	01/1998 $150 GR	$250-$300

(1998) Air Jordan 13 (XIII) Original

Picture:	Name:	Shoe Box:	Colorway:	Release Date/Retail Price/ Release Type	Market Value for DS (2013)
#440	Air Jordan 13 (XIII) Original "Bred"		Black/Varsity Red	1998 $150 GR	$320-$380

(1998) Air Jordan 13 (XIII) Original Low

Picture:	Name:	Shoe Box:	Colorway:	Release Date/Retail Price/ Release Type	Market Value for DS (2013)
#441	Air Jordan 13 (XIII) Original Low		Navy/ Metallic Silver/Black Carolina Blue	07/1998 $130 GR	$270-$290

(2004) Air Jordan 13 (XIII) Retro

Picture:	Name:	Shoe Box:	Colorway:	Release Date/Retail Price/ Release Type	Market Value for DS (2013)
#442	Air Jordan 13 (XIII) Retro "Wheat"		White/ Wheat	10/23/2004 $150 GR	$240-$270

(2004) Air Jordan 13 (XIII) Retro

Picture:	Name:	Shoe Box:	Colorway:	Release Date/Retail Price/ Release Type	Market Value for DS (2013)
#443	Air Jordan 13 (XIII) Retro "Bred" (PR: '98)		Black/ Varsity Red-White	12/22/2004 $150 GR	$320-$340

(2005) Air Jordan 13 (XIII) Retro

Picture:	Name:	Shoe Box:	Colorway:	Release Date/Retail Price/ Release Type	Market Value for DS (2013)
#444	Air Jordan 13 (XIII) Retro "Grey Toe"		White/ Maroon/ Grey	01/22/2005 $150 GR	$230-$260
#445	Air Jordan 13 (XIII) Retro "University Blue"		White/ Neutral Grey-University Blue	01/22/2005 $150 GR	$180-$220
#446	Air Jordan 13 (XIII) Retro (LS) "Altitude"		Black/ Altitude Green	02/26/2005 $150 Limited-Release	$240-$270

(2005) Air Jordan 13 (XIII) Retro

Picture:	Name:	Shoe Box:	Colorway:	Release Date/Retail Price/ Release Type	Market Value for DS (2013)
#447	Air Jordan 13 (XIII) Retro "Flint" (PR: '98)		French Blue University Blue-Flint Grey	04/19/2005 $150 GR	**$280-$310**

(2005) Air Jordan 13 (XIII) Retro Low

Picture:	Name:	Shoe Box:	Colorway:	Release Date/Retail Price/ Release Type	Market Value for DS (2013)
#448	Air Jordan 13 (XIII) Retro Low (LS) "Bobcat"		White/ Metallic Silver-Obsidian-Orange Flash	08/20/2005 $130 Limited-Release	**$150-$170**
#449	Air Jordan 13 (XIII) Retro Low		White/Black Varsity Maize	05/21/2005 $130 Limited-Release	**$180-$210**
#450	Air Jordan 13 (XIII) Retro Low		Black/White Varsity-Maize	05/21/2005 $130 Limited-Release	**$150-$180**

(2005) Air Jordan 13 (XIII) Retro Low

Picture:	Name:	Shoe Box:	Colorway:	Release Date/Retail Price/ Release Type	Market Value for DS (2013)
#451	Air Jordan 13 (XIII) Retro Low		White/Metallic Silver-Midnight Navy-Ice Blue	04/23/2005 $130 GR	$140-$160
#452	Air Jordan 13 (XIII) Retro "Bulls" Low (PR: '98)		White/Metallic Silver-Varsity Red-Black	04/23/2005 $130 GR	$160-$190

(2005) Air Jordan 13 (XIII) Retro Low

Picture:	Name:	Shoe Box:	Colorway:	Release Date/Retail Price/ Release Type	Market Value for DS (2013)
#453	(W) Air Jordan 13 (XIII) Retro Low		White/Carolina Blue/Pink	05/07/2005 $130 GR-Women	$80-$110

Fact
Michael Jordan would go on to win his 6th and last NBA championship during the 1997-1998 season.

(2008) Air Jordan 13 (XIII) Retro

Picture:	Name:	Shoe Box:	Colorway:	Release Date/Retail Price/ Release Type	Market Value for DS (2013)
#454	Air Jordan 13 (XIII) Retro (CDP) "He Got Game" (PR: '97)		White/Black-True Red	01/19/2008 $310 for Pack Limited-Release	$260-$290

(2010) Air Jordan 13 (XIII) Retro

Picture:	Name:	Shoe Box:	Colorway:	Release Date/Retail Price/ Release Type	Market Value for DS (2013)
#455	Air Jordan 13 (XIII) Retro Premio "BIN 23"		Team Red/Desert Clay-White	08/21/2010 N/A 1,734 Pairs released	$700-$800

Fact

When the Air Jordan 13 XIII's released in 1997-1998, it was also the same time Michael Jordan broke Kareem Abdul-Jabbar's NBA record for consecutive double digit games at 788th games.

(2010) Air Jordan 13 (XIII) Retro

Picture:	Name:	Shoe Box:	Colorway:	Release Date/Retail Price/ Release Type	Market Value for DS (2013)
#456	Air Jordan 13 (XIII) Retro "Altitude" (PR: '05)		Black/ Altitude Green	12/11/2010 $160 GR	$280-$310
#457	Air Jordan 13 (XIII) Retro "Flint" (PR: '98,'05)		French Blue University Blue-Flint Grey	11/26/2010 $160 GR	$270-$290
#458	Air Jordan 13 (XIII) Retro "Bulls" (PR: '98,'05)		White/ Black/True Red	12/18/2010 $160 GR	$190-$230

(2011) Air Jordan 13 (XIII) Retro

Picture:	Name:	Shoe Box:	Colorway:	Release Date/Retail Price/ Release Type	Market Value for DS (2013)
#459	Air Jordan 13 (XIII) Retro P.E. "Ray Allen"		White/ Clover/ Green	06/23/2011 $175 Limited Release	$500+

(2011) Air Jordan 13 (XIII) Retro

Picture:	Name:	Shoe Box:	Colorway:	Release Date/Retail Price/ Release Type	Market Value for DS (2013)
 #460	Air Jordan 13 (XIII) Retro "Playoff" (PR: '97)		Black/ Varsity Red-White-Vibrant Yellow	02/26/2011 $160 GR	$270-$290

Did you know?
In the movie "He Got Game", Jake Shuttlesworth, who is played by Denzel Washington, is seen wearing a pair of the Air Jordan 13 (XIII) throughout the movie.

Air Jordan 14 (XIV)

Air Jordan 14 (XIV)

The Air Jordan 14 (XIV) were the last Air Jordan model Jordan would wear during his time with the Chicago Bulls; he would retire for the second time at the end of the season. Although Nike created other shoes after the Air Jordan 14 (XIV), Jordan's retirement marked the end of an era in Chicago sports.

The shoes incoporated everything from a mock Ferrari logo, with the Jumpman inside of it, to side panel vents for additional "air conditioning" on your feet. Additionally, the shoes included seven Jumpman logos on each shoe to total 14 logos that symbolized the Air Jordan 14 (XIV).

(1998) Air Jordan 14 (XIV) Original

Picture:	Name:	Shoe Box:	Colorway:	Release Date/Retail Price/ Release Type	Market Value for DS (2013)
#461	Air Jordan 14 (XIV) Original "Black Toe"		White/Black Varsity Red	10/31/1998 $150 GR	**$250-$280**

(1999) Air Jordan 14 (XIV) Original

Picture:	Name:	Shoe Box:	Colorway:	Release Date/Retail Price/ Release Type	Market Value for DS (2013)
#462	Air Jordan 14 (XIV) Original "Candy Cane"		White/ Varsity Red/ Black	01/09/1999 $150 GR	**$190-$210**
#463	Air Jordan 14 (XIV) Original "Oxy"		White/Black Oxidized Green	02/13/1999 $150 GR	**$220-$250**
#464	Air Jordan 14 (XIV) Original "Last Shot"		Black/Black/ Varsity Red	03/27/1999 $150 GR	**$200-$230**

(1999) Air Jordan 14 (XIV) Original

Picture:	Name:	Shoe Box:	Colorway:	Release Date/Retail Price/ Release Type	Market Value for DS (2013)
#465	Air Jordan 14 (XIV) Original "Indiglo"		Black/Black White/ Indiglo	06/12/1999 $150 GR	$250-$270

(1999) Air Jordan 14 (XIV) Original Low

Picture:	Name:	Shoe Box:	Colorway:	Release Date/Retail Price/ Release Type	Market Value for DS (2013)
#466	Air Jordan 14 (XIV) Original Low "Columbia Blue"		White/ Columbia Blue/ Obsidian	08/04/1999 $130 GR	$150-$170
#467	Air Jordan 14 (XIV) Original Low "Royal"		Varsity Royal/Black/ White	06/23/1999 $130 GR	$240-$260
#468	Air Jordan 14 (XIV) Original Low "Ginger"		Light Ginger/ Black/White	09/15/1999 $130 GR	$240-$280

(2005) Air Jordan 14 (XIV) Retro

Picture:	Name:	Shoe Box:	Colorway:	Release Date/Retail Price/ Release Type	Market Value for DS (2013)
#469	Air Jordan 14 (XIV) Retro "Redwood"		Black/Light Graphite/ Metallic Silver/ Redwood	12/03/2005 $150 Limited-Release	$150-$170

(2005) Air Jordan 14 (XIV) Retro

Picture:	Name:	Shoe Box:	Colorway:	Release Date/Retail Price/ Release Type	Market Value for DS (2013)
#470	Air Jordan 14 (XIV) Retro "Last Shot" (PR: '99)		Black/Black/ Varsity Red	12/24/2005 $150 GR	$180-$210
#471	Air Jordan 14 (XIV) Retro		White/Linen Varsity Red	11/19/2005 $150 GR	$140-$150
#472	Air Jordan 14 (XIV) Retro "Forest Green"		White/ Forest Green/Light Graphite	10/22/2005 $150 GR	$160-$180

(2005) Air Jordan 14 (XIV) Retro

Picture:	Name:	Shoe Box:	Colorway:	Release Date/Retail Price/ Release Type	Market Value for DS (2013)
#473	(W) Air Jordan 14 (XIV) Retro		Black/Real Pink/ Metallic Silver	10/22/2005 $150 GR-Women	$130-$160
#474	Air Jordan 14 (XIV) Retro "Dark Cinder"		White/Dark Cinder/ Chutney	10/28/2005 $150 GR	$170-$210
#475	Air Jordan 14 (XIV) Retro		White/ Chartreuse/ Black	09/24/2005 $150 Limited-Release	$180-$210

(2005) Air Jordan 14 (XIV) Retro

Picture:	Name:	Shoe Box:	Colorway:	Release Date/Retail Price/ Release Type	Market Value for DS (2013)
#476	Air Jordan 14 (XIV) Retro		Light Graphite/ Chartreuse/ Black	09/24/2005 $150 Limited-Release	$190-$210

(2006) Air Jordan 14 (XIV) Retro

Picture:	Name:	Shoe Box:	Colorway:	Release Date/Retail Price/ Release Type	Market Value for DS (2013)
#477	Air Jordan 14 (XIV) Retro "Black Toe" (PR: '98)		White/Black Varsity Red/ Metallic Silver	04/18/2006 $150 GR	**$170-$190**
#478	Air Jordan 14 (XIV) Retro "Candy Cane" (PR: '99)		White/ Varsity Red/Black	01/14/2006 $150 GR	**$170-$200**
#479	Air Jordan 14 (XIV) Retro "University Blue"		Black/ University Blue/ Metallic Black	01/14/2006 $150 GR	**$150-$180**

(2006) Air Jordan 14 (XIV) Retro Low

Picture:	Name:	Shoe Box:	Colorway:	Release Date/Retail Price/ Release Type	Market Value for DS (2013)
#480	Air Jordan 14 (XIV) Retro Low		White/ Pacific Blue-MTS- Bright Ceramic	03/18/2006 $130 GR	**$70-$90**

(2006) Air Jordan 14 (XIV) Retro Low

Picture:	Name:	Shoe Box:	Colorway:	Release Date/Retail Price/ Release Type	Market Value for DS (2013)
 #481	(W) Air Jordan 14 (XIV) Retro Low		White/ Cerise- Classic Green	03/18/2006 $130 GR-Women	$70-$100

(2008) Air Jordan 14 (XIV) Retro

Picture:	Name:	Shoe Box:	Colorway:	Release Date/Retail Price/ Release Type	Market Value for DS (2013)
 #482	Air Jordan 14 (XIV) Retro (CDP)		Black/Varsity Red	03/15/2008 $310 for Pack Limited Release	$160-$180

(2011) Air Jordan 14 (XIV) Retro

Picture:	Name:	Shoe Box:	Colorway:	Release Date/Retail Price/ Release Type	Market Value for DS (2013)
	Air Jordan 14 (XIV) Retro		Light Graphite/ Midnight Navy- Black	10/08/2011 $160 GR	$160-$190

(2011) Air Jordan 14 (XIV) Retro

Picture:	Name:	Shoe Box:	Colorway:	Release Date/Retail Price/ Release Type	Market Value for DS (2013)
 #484	(GS) Air Jordan 14 (XIV) Retro		Black/Desert Pink	11/2011 $110 GS release	$100-$120
#485	Air Jordan 14 (XIV) Retro "Last Shot" (PR: '99,'05)		Black/Black/ Varsity Red	12/17/2011 $160 GR	$180-$200

(2012) Air Jordan 14 (XIV) Retro

Picture:	Name:	Shoe Box:	Colorway:	Release Date/Retail Price/ Release Type	Market Value for DS (2013)
 #486	(GS) Air Jordan 14 (XIV) Retro		White/Siren Red-Neptune Blue	03/17/2012 $110 GS release	$80-$90

Did you know?

The design behind the Air Jordan 14 (XIV) was based off the Ferrari 355F1, which Michael Jordan owned during his days as a Chicago Bulls player.

(2012) Air Jordan 14 (XIV) Retro

Picture:	Name:	Shoe Box:	Colorway:	Release Date/Retail Price/ Release Type	Market Value for DS (2013)
#487	Air Jordan 14 (XIV) Retro "Candy Cane" (PR: '99,'06)		White/ Varsity Red/Black	03/10/2012 $160 GR	$170-$200

Did you know?

The Air Jordan 14 (XIV) red/black colorway earned the nickname "The Last Shot" when Michael Jordan made the game winning basket against the Utah Jazz with 5.2 seconds left, inevitably earning the Chicago Bulls their 6th championship.

Beginning Moments Pack (BMP)

Picture:	Name:	Shoe Box:	Colorway:	Release Date/ Retail Price/ Release Type:	DS Market Value (2012)
	Air Jordan 1/1 "Old Love New Love" Beginning Moments Pack (BMP)		AJ 1 (I) "Old Loves" – White/Black – Varsity Red AJ 1 (I) "New Love" -Black/Varsity-Maize/White	04/24/2007 $200 for pack Limited-Released	$350-$380

Air Jordan Collezione Countdown Pack (CDP)

Picture:	Name:	Shoe Box:	Colorway:	Release Date/ Retail Price/ Release Type:	DS Market Value (2012)
	Air Jordan 1/22 Collezione Countdown Pack (CDP)		AJ 22 (XXII) – Black/White AJ 1 (I) -White/Varsity Red-Midnight Navy-Metallic Gold	09/20/2008 $310 Limited-Release	$290-$320
	Air Jordan 2/21 Collezione Countdown Pack (CDP)		AJ 2 (II) – Black/Varsity Red -Cement Grey AJ21 (XXI) -Black/Black – Dark Charcoal	04/26/2008 $310 Limited-Release	$320-$350

Air Jordan Collezione Countdown Pack (CDP)

Picture:	Name:	Shoe Box:	Colorway:	Release Date/ Retail Price/ Release Type:	DS Market Value (2012)
	Air Jordan 3/20 Collezione Countdown Pack (CDP)		AJ 3 (III) "Black Cement" - Black/Cement Grey AJ 20 (XX) - Black/Light Graphite	10/18/2008 $310 Limited-Release	$420-$440
	Air Jordan 4/19 Collezione Countdown Pack (CDP)		AJ 4 (IV) "Bred" - Black/Cement Grey-Fire Red AJ 19 (XIX) - Black/Chrome-Varsity Red	07/19/2008 $310 Limited-Release	$450-$470
	Air Jordan 5/18 Collezione Countdown Pack (CDP)		AJ 5 (V) "Fire Red" - White/Fire Red-Black AJ 18 (XVIII) - Black/Varsity Red	08/25/2008 $310 Limited-Release	$380-$420
	Air Jordan 6/17 Collezione Countdown Pack (CDP)		AJ 6 (VI) "Carmine" - White/Carmine-Black AJ 17 (XVII) - Black/Silver	05/14/2008 $310 Limited-Release	$530-$570

Air Jordan Collezione Countdown Pack (CDP)

Picture:	Name:	Shoe Box:	Colorway:	Release Date/ Retail Price/ Release Type:	DS Market Value (2012)
	Air Jordan 7/16 Collezione Countdown Pack (CDP)		AJ 7 (VII) "Hare"- White/Light Graphite-True Red AJ 16 (XVI) – Black/Varsity Red	06/21/2008 $310 Limited-Release	$440-$460
	Air Jordan 8/15 Collezione Countdown Pack (CDP)		AJ 8 (VIII) "Bugs Bunny" -White/Black/True-Red AJ 15 (XV) – Black/Varsity Red	11/08/2008 $310 Limited-Release	$380-$420
	Air Jordan 9/14 Collezione Countdown Pack (CDP)		AJ 9 (IX) "Playoff" -White/True Red-Black AJ 14 (XIV) – Black/Varsity Red	03/15/2008 $310 Limited-Release	$320-$350

Air Jordan Collezione Countdown Pack (CDP)

Picture:	Name:	Shoe Box:	Colorway:	Release Date/ Retail Price/ Release Type:	DS Market Value (2012)
	Air Jordan 10/13 Collezione Countdown Pack (CDP)		AJ 10 (X) "Shadow"- Black/Dark Shadow-Red AJ 13 (XIII) - "He Got Game" White/Black	01/19/2008 $310 Limited-Release	$440-$480
	Air Jordan 11/12 Collezione Countdown Pack (CDP)		AJ 11 (XI) -Black/True Red-White AJ 12 (XII) "Taxi" -Black/Black-	12/20/2008 $310 Limited-Release	$650-$680

Air Jordan Defining Moments Pack (DMP)

Picture:	Name:	Shoe Box:	Colorway:	Release Date/ Retail Price/ Release Type:	DS Market Value (2012)
	Air Jordan 11/6 Defining Moments Pack (DMP)		AJ 11 (XI) "Concords" - White/Metallic Gold-Black AJ 6 (VI) – Black/Metallic Gold	01/28/2006 $296 Limited-Release	$980-$1020 $900+

Air Jordan Defining Moments Pack (DMP)

Picture:	Name:	Shoe Box:	Colorway:	Release Date/ Retail Price/ Release Type:	DS Market Value (2012)
	Air Jordan 5 (V) Defining Moments Pack "Raging Bulls Pack" (DMP)		AJ 5 (V) "3M" Black/Varsity-Red AJ 5 (V) "Toro" – Varsity Red/Black	05/30/2009 $310 Pack Limited-Release	$750-$780 $740+
	Air Jordan 1 (I) Defining Moments Pack (60+) (DMP)		AJ 1 (I) "Bulls"- Black/Varsity Red AJ 1 (I) "Celtic" -White/Black-Celtic Green	07/11/2009 $225 Limited-Release	$420-$440
	Air Jordan 7 (VII) Defining Moments Pack (60+) (DMP)		AJ 7 (VII) "Raptor" - Black/Dark Charcoal-True Red AJ 7 (VII) "Magic" - White/Varsity Royal-Black	08/22/2009 $310 Limited-Release	$460-$490

Air Jordan Golden Moments Pack (GMP)

Picture:	Name:	Shoe Box:	Colorway:	Release Date/ Retail Price/ Release Type:	DS Market Value (2012)
	Air Jordan 6/7 Golden Moments Pack (GMP)		**AJ 6 (VI)** - White/ Metallic Gold **AJ 7 (VII)** - Black/ Metallic Gold	08/18/2012 $350 Limited-Release	$420-$440

Air Jordan Infrared Pack

Picture:	Name:	Shoe Box:	Colorway:	Release Date/ Retail Price/ Release Type:	DS Market Value (2012)
	Air Jordan 6 (VI) Infrared Pack		AJ 6 (VI) – Black/Black Infra-red AJ 6 (VI) – White/Infra-red-Black	06/19/2010 $310 Limited-Release	$640-$670

Made in the USA
Charleston, SC
05 April 2013